"We can no longer be the silent moral majority sitting idly watching our world be corrupted and taken over by the immoral minority."

"Integrity is when our thoughts, words, and actions are in harmony with each other. Moral Integrity is when all three are aligned with righteous principles and actions."

"The people of the world are tired of morally bankrupt leaders who focus on their own personal gain."

"Evil attempts to control and enslave us, but God in on our side, and God wins."

"No man, or Institution created by man, has any right to take away or infringe on our Personal Freedom."

"Like a rudder on a ship, it only takes a small, determined force to make a big change in direction."

"Good men and women fortified with correct principles and committed to living them, are a powerful force to be reckoned with."

"Our grandchildren are counting on us to hand the baton of freedom to them, fully intact, so they can enjoy life, liberty, and the pursuit of happiness."

"The cause of Freedom is just, and the world needs your unique contribution."

Matthew J Cameron

Engaged Patriots Manifesto

Living These 10 Values Will Save
Our Families and Communities

Matthew J Cameron

ISBN 979-8-9883185-1-4 (Hardback)
ISBN 979-8-9883185-0-7 (Paperback)
ISBN 979-8-9883185-2-1 (eBook)
ISBN 979-8-9883185-4-5 (AudioBook)

TABLE OF CONTENTS

DEDICATION I
ABOUT THE AUTHOR III
INTRODUCTION I
ENGAGED PATRIOTS MANIFESTO V
WE ARE DESTINED FOR GREATNESS ....- 1 -
WE SHALL PROTECT THE WEAK AND INNOCENT ....- 8 -

WE SHALL PROTECT THE WEAK AND INNOCENT CHALLENGE ...... - 17 -

WE SHALL SHOW COMPASSION ....- 18 -

WE SHALL SHOW COMPASSION CHALLENGE .... - 26 -

WE SHALL TEACH CORRECT PRINCIPLES.........................- 27 -

WE SHALL TEACH CORRECT PRINCIPLES CHALLENGE .... - 40 -

WE SHALL STRENGTHEN OUR FAMILIES.........................- 41 -

WE SHALL STRENGTHEN OUR FAMILIES CHALLENGE .... - 51 -

WE SHALL SERVE IN OUR COMMUNITIES ....- 52 -

WE SHALL SERVE IN OUR COMMUNITIES CHALLENGE .... - 60 -

WE SHALL REBUILD OUR ECONOMIES ....- 61 -

WE SHALL REBUILD OUR ECONOMIES – SMALL BUSINESS CHALLENGE
.... - 86 -

WE SHALL FEAR NO OPPRESSOR ....- 87 -

WE SHALL FEAR NO OPPRESSOR CHALLENGE .... - 94 -

WE SHALL LEAD WITH INTEGRITY..................................- 95 -

WE SHALL LEAD WITH INTEGRITY CHALLENGE....................... - 102 -

WE SHALL HONOR GOD ....- 103 -

WE SHALL HONOR GOD CHALLENGE .... - 111 -

WE SHALL LEAVE A LEGACY OF FREEDOM .... - 112 -

WE SHALL LEAVE A LEGACY OF FREEDOM CHALLENGE............ - 117 -

ARE YOU READY TO LEAD? .... - 118 -
A BRIGHTER VISION .... - 121 -
WHY ENGAGED PATRIOTS? .... - 128 -
HELLO PATRIOTS! .... - 136 -
ENGAGED PATRIOTS MANIFESTO - ASSESSMENT .... - 141 -
21 PRINCIPLES ASSESSMENT .... - 147 -
FAMILY ASSESSMENT TOOL .... - 153 -
SPIRITUALITY ASSESSMENT .... - 170 -
DECLARATION OF INDEPENDENCE .... - 177 -
BILL OF RIGHTS .... - 188 -

AMENDMENT I .... - 188 -
AMENDMENT II .... - 188 -
AMENDMENT III .... - 188 -
AMENDMENT IV .... - 188 -
AMENDMENT V .... - 189 -
AMENDMENT VI .... - 189 -
AMENDMENT VII .... - 189 -
AMENDMENT VIII .... - 190 -
AMENDMENT IX .... - 190 -
AMENDMENT X .... - 190 -

SO, ASK YOURSELF THE FOLLOWING QUESTIONS: ...... - 191 -

DEDICATION

This book is dedicated to my sweet wife, Gina, our six wonderful children, and eight awesome grandchildren. We love you more than words can express and intend to leave you with a better world.

ABOUT THE AUTHOR

My name is Matthew J Cameron. I am not an Author. I am not a Writer. I am not Famous. I am a Son, Brother, Husband, Father, Grandfather, and Patriot. I felt compelled to write this book. It comes from my heart. I wrote it for my children and grandchildren.

INTRODUCTION

During my lifetime, I have seen our nation fall from grace. Once a beacon of hope to the world, we have lost our moral compass. Our leaders have been corrupted by money and power. Our cities have become infected with degenerative behavior. Crime and drug use is out of control. Illegal aliens flood our borders. People do not feel safe. Polarization in politics and lifestyles is causing contention and chaos. Economic turmoil is destroying our wealth and increasing our stress levels. Good people have been silent as we watched our world disintegrate before our eyes. These problems have been caused by a small group of evil people who want to destroy our freedoms and our country.

My hope is that we, the Silent but Moral Majority, can combat the evil that is growing around us by creating a grass roots movement of patriots who are committed to restoring the Principles and Freedoms that we all hold dear.

We must start with ourselves and recommit to be better people. We must embrace the correct principles that have been the basis of all free societies. We must be honest, virtuous, and hard working. We must take personal responsibility for our actions and be accountable for any consequences. We must teach our children and grandchildren to do the same.

The ten declarations in the Engaged Patriots Manifesto are based on common sense and time-tested principles. They are a statement of both our values and a proposed action plan that can serve as a guide in our daily lives.

This book is not intended as a casual read, to be easily forgotten. No, it is my hope that we embrace and implement these declarations in our individual lives and, in so doing, affect real change in the world!

We must expand our reach and service to those around us in ever-increasing circles of influence for good. We must be bold as we face the evils of our day. We must stand for what's right, even in the face of intimidation and social oppression from woke corporations, controlled media, and friends who have been brainwashed by decades of propaganda.

Satan is stirring up his wrath and making his power play for the souls of men, but God has given us the power to overcome him. The battleground is clear; God has given us Freedom and Personal Agency, and Satan wants to take them away, control all aspects of our lives, and lead us down the path to total captivity.

He influences those who crave money and power to do his bidding. He promises them more money, power, and fame. He convinces them that they are part of the elite, deserving of more than others. He convinces them that we should be subject to their will, and they should have power over us. He convinces them that our lives are not as valuable as theirs. He convinces them that there are limited resources on the earth, and they need to horde them for themselves and limit our access. In return for money, power, and fame, he demands his followers implement his plans for the children of God.

So, while we have been busy living our lives and supporting our families, he has been busy creating a web of lies and control that has slowly been tightening around us.

Introduction

This battle between good and evil is not new. It has been raging since the beginning of time here on Earth. However, as we get closer to the end times, Satan is ramping up his efforts as he makes his final push to destroy all the good things that God wants for us and impose his will upon us.

Being aware is the first critical step. Once aware, we must begin immediately to combat his evil plans in our everyday lives. We can no longer be the Silent Moral Majority sitting idly, watching our world be corrupted and taken over by the Immoral Minority. It is time for righteous indignation.

The weak-minded and corrupt among us have fallen for his lies! They like to hide in the shadows as they do his bidding. They fear being exposed. We must shine light on them and their evil deeds. We must hold them accountable for their actions.

> **❝ We can no longer be the Silent Moral Majority sitting idly watching our world be corrupted and taken over by the Immoral Minority.**

We will teach others and be examples of goodness and service. We will create a groundswell that will be hard for evil to overcome.

Join with us as we embrace this important work to Strengthen our Families and Communities.

We are on God's side, and God will prevail!

ENGAGED PATRIOTS MANIFESTO

1. We Shall Protect the Weak and Innocent.
2. We Shall Show Compassion to Others.
3. We Shall Teach Correct Principles.
4. We Shall Strengthen our Families.
5. We Shall Serve in Our Communities.
6. We Shall Rebuild Our Economies.
7. We Shall Fear No Oppressor.
8. We Shall Lead With Integrity.
9. We Shall Honor God.
10. We Shall Leave a Legacy of FREEDOM.

Take our Engaged Patriots Manifesto – Personal Assessment
(located in the back of the book)

Engaged Patriots Manifesto

Or take our online Assessment

WE ARE DESTINED FOR GREATNESS

Each of us has planted deep inside the seed of Greatness. Each of us are a divine living soul. Our soul is a combination of an eternal spirit and a mortal body. We each have a conscience … which gives us an innate understanding of right and wrong. We are also endowed with the gift of agency, the ability to make personal choices as we live our lives. With agency comes personal responsibility and accountability. We can only be held accountable if we are free to exercise our agency.

As sons and daughters of our Creator, we each have the potential to become like Him as we emulate His character traits in our own lives by making good decisions each day.

> **"** Each of us has planted deep inside the seed of Greatness.

Our natural desire to grow, achieve, and contribute was planted in our souls by our Creator. We are all architects and engineers as we design and create the world around us. Just consider the sense of satisfaction you feel after finishing a project and stepping back to admire your work.

Though we might sometimes be impressed by our own creations, we must stand in awe at God's creations. God's creations are amazing, the beauty of the mountains and the seas, the intensity of a thunder and lightning storm, the incredible colors of a sunset, the peace and beauty of a new fallen snow. We were given all these things to enjoy as we live our lives here on Earth. But we also have a responsibility to be good stewards over the Earth and to treat our brothers and sisters with love and respect.

How we choose to follow these principles is an important part of the test of this mortal life. Therefore, the right to choose, to make our own decisions, is at the center of our humanity. Anytime we experience social oppression, it infringes on our right to choose. And social oppression comes in many forms and levels of severity.

Consider the social pressure that a teenager feels from their peer group. At that time in life, friends are more influential and important to them than their own parents and siblings. The pressure to conform is immense. It takes a strong individual to stand up to the group and influence them to make good decisions. You would expect adults to be less prone to this pressure, but the fear of rejection and social scorning is often too much for many to bear. They quickly cave into the social pressure of the larger group.

Another observation I have made is that, once they cave to the social pressure, they become staunch advocates for the positions they recently opposed. But lowering our standards to the lowest common denominator in society will never help any of us reach our potential.

Attempting to control others at any level also goes against the personal freedom that God granted each of us. We value and guard our own freedom but often make demands on others that infringe on their freedom to choose.

When in a position of authority or leadership, we must be careful that we provide guidance and direction but that we do not force or coerce others into the behaviors that we want. To be a leader, you must have willing followers. Weak leaders use social oppression to get what they want.

Totalitarianism is a severe example of social oppression. It comes with many labels—socialism, fascism, communism, etc. But, in any form, the intent is to control others with restrictive policies and force to ensure that the minority in power stays in power and that the productivity of the people is diverted to lavishly support this controlling class. When people's freedoms and liberties are suppressed, their potential for greatness may be temporarily restrained. But their innate desire to be free will always overcome the forces that attempt to control and oppress.

We must never voluntarily give up our freedoms and liberties in exchange for safety and security or we will end up with neither. Our freedoms and liberties can be at risk because we either willingly give them up, are coerced to give them up, or we become so complacent that they are taken away and we fail to notice until it is too late. Once gone, future generations will not even be aware of what they have lost!

Most people willing accept the reality that they are presented with. We must always question why and push back against social oppression in all its forms if we are to maintain our freedoms that allow us to learn, grow, and achieve greatness in our lives.

The world teaches us that scarcity is the normal condition of humanity. If I achieve something, it must be at your expense. In sports, there is always a winner and a loser. The winners go home, elated; and the losers wallow in their loss or get more motivated to win next time. In business, we often bid for contracts or compete for market share. In war, the winner gets all the spoils, and the losers pay the price with their property, freedom, and often their lives.

We talk about the survival of the fittest and natural selection. These are all constructs of man. God teaches us that, in His Kingdom, there are many mansions and enough space there for all who are obedient and worthy to be in His presence. He teaches us that abundance will be the normal condition in eternity.

We see the principle of abundance everywhere in the world around us. For example, astronomists have determined that the universe is expanding in all directions at a rapid pace. The natural state of all creation is to grow and expand. All life in the biosphere, when provided with the basic ingredients for life, will grow and expand. Trade in free markets will expand, and all market participants will benefit from the variety of products and services, and increased trade. Growth is natural, growth is good, growth creates abundance for all.

> **❝** Love grows to encompass all who live under its protection.

Love is another example of the principle of abundance. When you first fall in love with your spouse or partner, you feel such a connection and love for them that it is hard to imagine loving anyone else that much. But then you have children, and when you see your child for the first time, you instantly have a love for them that is almost unexplainable. It doesn't reduce or diminish your love for your spouse; your love just increases to include both. And then, when your second child is on the way, you think: how can I love another child as much as my first? Then they arrive, and your love for them is just as strong. It is not that they each get half of your love. No, your love grows to include both! Love grows to encompass all who live under its protection.

Once we embrace the idea of abundance, we will no longer feel that we are competing with others for limited resources, and we will unlock our ability to bless the lives of others.

Abundance is one of the key principles that will allow us to achieve Greatness in our lives. As Sons and Daughters of our Creator, we each have the potential to become like Him in character and deed. This is a realization that should strengthen our resolve to improve each day.

> **"** Greatness is measured in the character traits we develop as we work and serve others.

Greatness is not defined by the scope or impact of our contributions to the world. Greatness is measured in the character traits we develop as we work and serve others.

Are we kind and compassionate? Can we be depended on to keep our word? Do we carry our share of the workload and stay on a task until it is completed? Do we share our skills and talents with others? Do our words match our actions? Do we lead by example? It is all these small decisions that we make every day that become our habits that lead to our character traits that will determine our eternal destiny. Greatness is, therefore, the sum of all the good decisions and choices we make.

Now, imagine a world where everyone can unlock their potential and create and innovate in ways that bless the entire human race. A world where value delivered is rewarded fairly in the marketplace. A world where everyone has access to resources and opportunities to contribute. A world where each of our unique talents and gifts can be shared. This is a world of freedom. This is a world of abundance, not scarcity. Scarcity creates fear; abundance creates hope.

> **"** Like a rudder on a ship, it only takes a small, determined force to make a big change in direction.

Together, we can create this world. It starts with the silent majority, frustrated by the current state of the world, engaging their minds, channeling their energies, and applying their resources to reestablish personal freedom, drive innovation, rebuild the economy, and ensure a better world for our children and grandchildren. Like a rudder on a ship, it only takes a small, determined force to make a big change in direction.

Our founding fathers created this amazing land of opportunity we call America while under severe oppression with limited resources against the most powerful military in the world! Can we not step up and defend this amazing gift? If you are willing, your help is needed!

Both now and in the eternities to come, We are Destined For Greatness.

WE SHALL PROTECT THE WEAK AND INNOCENT

Evil preys on the innocent; criminals' prey on the weak.

I recall an interview that was done with a hardened criminal. He was shown a series of pictures of people and asked who he would choose to attack. He consistently chose people who were old, weak, or distracted. Much like the lion on the savannah, they have their best chance of success with these three groups.

When society attaches minor penalties for these behaviors, then we can expect to see more of these crimes, and the criminal class will flourish. For far too long, we have allowed this to continue! We must have zero tolerance for the abuse of these tender souls.

> " Nobody controls another by mistake. No, it is a deliberate decision made with full intent.

Throughout the ages, evil people have oppressed the weak. They take whatever advantage they have—physical strength, economic might, or political power—and they use it to oppress and control the weak and innocent. Countless children are mentally and physically abused. Countless women are beaten and raped. Countless people are enslaved by the systems of control created by those evil few without moral integrity.

Control in all forms is an affront to God. He gave us our agency and personal freedoms, and those who seek to take them away will be accountable to God for their actions. Nobody controls another by mistake. No, it is a deliberate decision made with full intent. God knows our hearts and minds and there will be no excuse for these behaviors.

Thomas Jefferson's personal motto was "Rebellion to Tyrants is Obedience to God." That should be the rallying cry to all of us as we seek to repel the evil forces we encounter.

> **"** Thomas Jefferson's personal motto was "Rebellion to Tyrants is Obedience to God."

As men and women of strong moral character, we must be vigilant in protecting those who are not able to protect themselves. We must keep a careful watch for those with evil intent. They lurk in the shadows, waiting for an opportunity to strike. Waiting to take from others for their own personal gain. They steal personal property which the owners worked hard to purchase. They violate rights of personal security and peace. They physically attack and intimidate with their violent crimes. They steal innocence and personal dignity from rape victims. They steal personal freedom from human trafficking victims. They leave in their wake fear, shame, and hopelessness.

Fortunately, they are the minority. By most estimates, they represent only 3-5% of the population.

This group has embraced evil and has managed to suppress their conscience to the point they feel no regret for their evil deeds. They often use physical force to gain advantage over their victims.

This is one of the key reasons why our founding fathers codified the right to "Keep and Bear Arms" in our Second Amendment to the Constitution. They knew that both tyrants with armies, and lone criminals, could be kept in check if the populace remains armed. It is not surprising that those who wish to control us continually argue to remove this right by pointing to the criminals who commit mass shootings or violent crimes as reasons to take our guns, as if that will somehow make everyone safe. This is flawed logic from the start.

Criminals will have guns no matter what, as it turns out they don't obey laws, and it is only the moral majority, armed with guns, who keep them in check.

Over the past few years, many brave citizens have foiled the plans of the criminals by acting quickly to counter their attacks. There should not be any restrictions that limit our ability to Keep and Bear Arms at all times and in all places to protect ourselves, our loved ones, and anyone else in harm's way.

When the evil and criminally inclined believe we, the Moral Majority, will remain passive, they are emboldened to be more aggressive. They commit atrocities in broad daylight, and they mock our resolve to keep peace in our communities. They must be made aware that we will not stand idly by as they commit their crimes against our elderly, our women, and our children.

Recently, in Brazil, an off-duty policewoman stopped a criminal who pulled out his gun and was going to attack several women and children. The off-duty policewoman acted quickly and took the perpetrator down before he could inflict any harm.

The attacker was completely shocked that their crime didn't go as planned. He was both wailing in pain from the multiple gunshot wounds and screaming in disbelief that he was the one who had been shot! It was an incredible act of bravery and, hopefully, a powerful lesson to all would-be criminals that good people will not stand by watching and let them get away with their crimes. Great is the shock on their faces when they are met with equal or greater force. Just like bullies in the playground, the criminal often runs or cowers in weakness when confronted.

Financial crimes are another way that criminals take advantage of the weak and innocent. The result can be just as devastating as a physical attack.

Many elderly people have had their life savings stolen through acts of fraud or coercion. Countless innocent and trusting people have fallen for investment schemes, identity scams, and cyber-crimes. Much of this is organized crime or nation state actors, working at an industrial scale. Truly, evil has permeated modern society as never before.

In addition to vigilance from the moral majority, our laws must be enforced to have the desired effect. The criminals must understand that the consequences of their actions will not be waived, and that justice will be swift for their crimes.

Countries that have strict laws on crime tend to have little crime. We must have penalties that act as a strong deterrent to would be criminals.

Recently, in liberal states and cities, lenient laws are being passed that encourage illegal behaviors. Liberal attorney generals and judges are also applying lenient policies as they enforce the laws. For example, in San Francisco, they allow shoplifting up to $1,000 without any prosecution whatsoever. As you would expect from such a lenient and immoral policy, shoplifting has skyrocketed. Criminals walk in, take whatever they want, and walk out with a smile on their face in broad daylight. This is legalized theft! Many stores have had to close due to this policy.

One of the key principles that free societies are based on is property rights. The right to own and keep the property you have acquired through legal means. When the government steps in and decides how to redistribute the property of one citizen and arbitrarily give it to another, they are violating this core principle and destabilizing our society.

 Government only has three jobs:

1. Provide security for the citizens.
2. Enforce laws and property rights.
3. Provide public services.

During the summer riots of 2020, rioters burned and looted extensively in many US cities. The media told us they were "mostly peaceful" protests. We could clearly see with our own eyes that this was a complete lie.

Governments not only allowed the chaos, but they actually encouraged it by defunding police departments in advance of the riots. These riots could have been easily stopped with local police forces or aid from the national guard, but governors and mayors allowed it to happen. Not only were lives lost, but many businesses were burned down and permanently closed.

Government only has three jobs:

1. Provide security for the citizens.
2. Enforce laws and property rights.
3. Provide public services.

They are failing the people on every front! Our infrastructure is in ruins, cities are unsafe, and laws favor the criminals.

The worst crimes committed against the weak and innocent are human trafficking and the sex slave trade. It is estimated that there are nearly 25 million people in forced labor, including 16 million in the private economy, and 4.8 million in forced sexual exploitation on the planet today. All of these people have been stripped of their basic human right of personal freedom. Estimates are that 20-30% of these victims were sold or recruited by friends or family members.

It is hard to imagine the horrors these victims endure year after year. The other thing that is hard to grasp is that the supply of slaves is driven by strong demand! What kind of sick people would purchase another human being and subject them to such cruel treatment? They have completely lost their conscience somewhere along the way. There must be a special place in hell for these evil people!

We have a modern-day hero, Tim Ballard, who is doing something about this. He created Operation Underground Railroad, an organization that rescues the victims of human trafficking and sex trades while providing support to help them get reestablished in a new life. It is not enough to simply rescue them if they do not have the means to start a new life in a safe environment.

Tim describes rescuing children in cages and looking into their scared eyes. They don't understand why these things are happening to them, and they are helpless on their own to change their circumstances. He has children of his own, and it breaks his heart to see these innocent victims. But what joy it gives him to release them from the clutches of these evil people. Tim truly exemplifies the first declaration of our Manifesto: We Shall Protect the Weak and Innocent.

There is much to be done to eradicate human slavery and sex trafficking from the Earth, and more good people are needed to help with this noble effort.

It is comforting to know that all these horrible crimes will be punished either in this life or in the eternities to come. No one can hide from God, and no one will get away with their sins. But it must break God's heart to witness how evil some of His children have become.

> **"** No one can hide from God, and no one will get away with their sins.

It will also be a harsh reality for good people when they learn that many senior leaders in our governments, social institutions, media, and large corporations have succumbed to the desire for money and power and are controlled by higher-up elites who directly worship Satan.

These corrupt leaders, who we have trusted, have been working directly against the best interests of We the People. They have undermined our economy, compromised our national security, allowed drugs to flood into our country, and corrupted our youth. They have facilitated human trafficking and taken down foreign governments who oppose them. We have all been victims of their greed and corruption. In a real sense we have been the weak and innocent they oppress. These are bold accusations, but the evidence to support these claims is deep and conclusive, and easily accessible by any who want to learn for themselves.

Our founding fathers would be shocked to learn that, even with the protections they put in place to shield us from tyrants, these evil people have still managed to infiltrate our ranks, rise to the top of our institutions, and gained power over us.

However, while we believe in consequences for actions and justice for crimes, as good people, we also believe in mercy. We believe in repentance and second chances. Everyone makes mistakes and falls short, but when we repent and give restitution for our sins, we will be forgiven. Our hope for criminals is that, once they have paid the price for their crimes, they will have a change of heart, real remorse, and a desire to live better lives, to embrace correct principles, spend their efforts on legitimate pursuits, employ their skills creating value, and join with the rest of us in becoming contributing members of society. This may be wishful thinking, but God grants everyone many opportunities to repent and become better people, even those who attempt to oppress and control us.

We are many; they are few. God is on our side, and until the final judgment, He is counting on us to do our part.

Therefore, We Shall Protect the Weak and Innocent.

WE SHALL PROTECT THE WEAK AND INNOCENT CHALLENGE

1. Identify ten potential circumstances where you might have an opportunity to protect the weak or innocent.
2. Write out your pre-planned response to each situation.
3. Write a short note of gratitude to someone who helped you or a family member in the past.
4. List an example of a time you failed to serve when the opportunity arose and how you felt afterward.
5. Write a commitment statement detailing how you will respond when future opportunities arise.

WE SHALL SHOW COMPASSION

Compassion is an emotion involving a sense of caring and understanding for the suffering of others. It is often accompanied by a willingness to help those in need or in distress.

Jesus Christ is a great example of compassion for all. He never hesitated to stop and lift another. We have many examples of this in the scriptures where His disciples were concerned that He would be inconvenienced by the many requests for His attention, but Jesus always took the time to respond with love and compassion. He was always willing to leave the ninety-nine to help the one in need. It was only afterward that Jesus' disciples saw the results of his compassionate acts and understood His deep love for God's children.

In the story of cleansing the ten lepers, it is interesting that only one returned to thank Him. His comment "were there not ten?" showed His disappointment for their apparent lack of gratitude for this blessing. This is a key lesson for all who are on the receiving end of compassion.

My maternal grandparents were great examples of love and service to everyone they met. My grandfather was born of immigrant Italian parents and was the first generation born in America. His father worked in various mines throughout the Western United States. They eventually settled in Butte Montana, a tough mining town.

My grandmother was born of Pioneer heritage with her grandparents having crossed the plains in the mid-1850s to settle in Salt Lake City. They were both hard working and spent all their spare time serving those around them. They both loved to cook and provided many meals for friends and relatives. They visited the elderly and the sick on a regular basis.

My grandfather was always helping others with projects around their homes. He would walk around the neighborhood, looking for jobs that needed to be done then just start doing them. As a result of his constant service, he developed many close friendships.

Once, when he needed a new roof, his friends surprised him by returning the service he had often given them. While he was at work, they came over and completely reroofed his house. When he got home and saw what they had done, he just stood there and cried tears of gratitude.

> **"** It is rare to share a smile and not receive one in return. Kindness is contagious!

We can begin to model this in our own lives as we become more aware of those around us. Look for people in need and offer an uplifting hand. There will be opportunities every day if we look for them. It may be as simple as opening the door for someone with their hands full, providing a listening ear to someone in need, or showing gratitude for those who serve you! A smile is free, but it can uplift another who is having a rough day. It is rare to share a smile and not receive one in return. Kindness is contagious!

Consider this thought experiment. Be honest with yourself. When you pass a homeless person on the street, what is your first thought? Are you scared? Are you disgusted with their appearance? Do you pity them? Do you want to help them? Our instinctual reactions are a good indication of our current level of compassion. If our immediate thought is to help them, setting aside our own current priorities, then we lean toward compassion.

Second question: what do you do in that moment? Do you keep walking, or act immediately on your first thought? Making quick decisions in these moments will reinforce this important trait in our lives and strengthen our resolve to be a force for good in this world.

Try this simple experiment with the next person you meet. Smile at them, ask how their day is going. Listen to their response, and then respond with empathy and compassion. Everyone has a story; everyone has daily challenges and frustrations. I predict you will make a genuine connection that surprises both of you.

We all need to make connections with others. It is an important part of being human. Babies who are abandoned or neglected will die from lack of love and connection before they die from malnutrition. Many who commit suicide are lonely; they feel unloved or unneeded. They lose all hope for real connections with others, and they want to end the pain this is causing them.

The Golden Gate Bridge in San Francisco is one of the top suicide locations in the United States. Hundreds jump to their death each year. Few survive the 265-foot drop to the water.

There is a peculiar phenomenon that has become a tradition among jumpers. They always leave their shoes on the bridge. They want someone to find their shoes and know that they jumped! They want to be remembered! It is heartbreaking to think about the loneliness and pain that they must be feeling in those last moments of life. If only one of us could have been there to show love and compassion in their critical moment of need!

Being more aware of other's feelings and needs can give us many opportunities to serve. We can be the answer to help relieve their pain through connecting and showing compassion. Just imagine the good that we can do if each of us were to do one small act of compassion each day. Billions of acts of service every day! This one principle could do more to bring peace and harmony to our troubled world than any other.

Showing love to others through small, compassionate acts would restore hope with even the most cynical, and through the law of reciprocity encourage everyone to do the same.

> **"** Being more aware of other's feelings and needs can give us many opportunities to serve.

As we expand our desire to help others, we will find many opportunities to support more formal causes. From local soup kitchens to international efforts to bring clean water and electricity to remote villages, there are many options to give service.

Our family has been blessed to participate in some of these projects. We have worked hand in hand with local villagers, planting gardens, building stoves for their homes, installing water lines to their villages, or creating simple grain milling operations that free up the women from hours of hand-grinding grains each day to feed their families. It is always amazing to me the level of connection that we develop with the villagers during these short expeditions. Even with the language barriers, deep love and gratitude are felt by all. The final day is always tough, with many tears flowing as we part ways.

Recently, on an expedition to Peru, the villagers made us promise to never forget them. The village children ran alongside our buses, holding out their hands and crying as we drove away!

I am always impressed how some have dedicated their entire lives to compassionate service for others. As mentioned earlier, Operation Underground Railroad is working to give back freedom to individuals who are victims of human trafficking. I am certain there is a cause that will pull at your heartstrings, too.

> " I am certain there is a cause that will pull at your heartstrings.

For me, it has always been concern for the plight of innocent children. They often suffer for problems they didn't create, don't understand, and are helpless to change. I particularly have a soft spot for children without parents to support them.

Humans need many years of love and support before we can be on our own. The odds are stacked heavily against children who have been abandoned or orphaned at a young age.

When my wife and I discovered that many young Thai girls are sold into sexual slavery at the age of twelve, we were outraged and decided we could do something to help. While we already had two awesome boys and could have more birth children, we began to check into adoption opportunities. We were matched up with a little baby girl who was just turning one. Her mother was only seventeen and, while away at school, got pregnant. Her parents never even knew she had given birth to a daughter.

After eighteen months of legal paperwork, we were able to travel to Thailand and pick her up. By that time, she was two and a half and was speaking Thai well. What an abrupt change for this little girl to be sent to the other side of the world, into a new environment where none of us spoke Thai and she had to learn to speak English.

The first six months were hard for her. She couldn't communicate with us and, at random times, she would drop to the ground and just start crying. But once she learned English, she began to thrive. She is now a beautiful woman, twenty-eight years old and married to a good man.

Four years later, we felt like there was another little girl out there who we needed to adopt. We found a baby of six months who had been abandoned by her mother at the hospital. Her mother was living on the streets and already had three other children who would beg on the street corners each day. We were able to expedite the process and pick her up after only nine months of legal paperwork.

She just graduated from college and, at twenty-four years old, is both beautiful and smart. We are so proud of both. We are also grateful that we have had the opportunity to raise these two beautiful girls and give them a better chance in life.

Another four years later, we felt a tug on our hearts and adopted a third girl, this time from Kazakhstan. She lived in a forgotten orphanage behind an abandoned mining operation, thirty miles outside of Jezkazgan, Kazakhstan. The town was the most depressing I have ever seen. After eighty years of Soviet rule, the people were dejected and hopeless. None of them smiled.

The orphanage was even more depressing. It consisted of two buildings—the baby house where the kids lived until they turned eight, and the adolescent house at the back of the property where they lived until they were kicked out at age sixteen. When the eight-year-old girls were transferred to the adolescent house, their initiation was to be gang-raped by all the boys in the house.

There were sixteen girls in the adolescent house. Our little girl had just turned eight by the time we got all the legal paperwork done and were able to travel to Kazakhstan, but we didn't get there in time to save her from this experience. These boys caused a lot of damage to her little female parts. I was both furious and sad.

Once these kids were transferred to the adolescent house, they were assumed to be too old to be adopted. The other girls looked longingly as they knew they would not be rescued. We desperately wanted to bring them all home with us. There was one little nine-year-old girl, Christina, a blonde-haired, blue-eyed Russian girl who I can still picture in my mind's eye; she haunts my dreams to this day. These kids deserved a better chance in life, and it broke my heart to leave them in that awful place.

Shortly after we left, the adoption program was cancelled when one of the team members from the adoption agency was murdered for the large amount of cash he carried related to the adoptions. God only knows what happened to the other children.

Millions of children around the world face similar plights. I have always thought that if families each adopted one or two of these kids, we could solve this problem so quickly and get them in good homes where they would be safe, loved, and have a chance for a healthy and productive life.

As we each step out of our personal bubbles and look around, we will be surprised that there are others in need everywhere we go. With greater awareness comes more opportunities to show compassion. We don't need to try to save the whole world tomorrow. Start small and increase your efforts as your time and resources allow.

Compassion is our opportunity for God to work through us.

Therefore, We Shall Show Compassion.

WE SHALL SHOW COMPASSION CHALLENGE

1. List ten situations where you might have an opportunity to show compassion.
2. List three situations from the past where you were proud of your response and describe the feeling you had afterward.
3. Write a short note to a person who has shown you or a family member compassion in the past.
4. List three situations where you had an opportunity to serve but failed to act on your prompting.
5. Write a commitment statement on how you will serve when future opportunities arise.

WE SHALL TEACH CORRECT PRINCIPLES

Throughout the ages and across all religions and wisdom literature, several core moral principles have emerged. These principles guide our behavior and, when applied in our families and communities, bring peace and prosperity to all. The following list, though admittedly incomplete, should serve us well.

1. **Speak the Truth.** Speaking the truth means communicating accurately and honestly about facts, opinions, and feelings. It includes being honest and straightforward in your words and actions, and not intentionally misleading or deceiving others. The complement to speaking the truth is being open to hearing the truth from others and being willing to accept it if it rings true to you.

2. **Honor Your Commitments.** Honoring your commitments involves taking steps to ensure you fulfill your commitments. This includes setting a timeline, breaking down tasks into manageable chunks, and setting goals. Additionally, it involves being open and honest about your progress and communicating delays in a timely manner. You must also be willing to ask for help if needed.

3. **Seek Wisdom.** Wisdom can be sought in many ways. Reading the wisdom literature, studying the lives of great

people, and talking to wise people who have knowledge and experience are all great ways to get started. Cultivating a readiness to learn and an openness to new ideas and perspectives is another way to seek wisdom. Finally, taking time to reflect and meditate is a powerful way to gain clarity and insight.

4. **Take Responsibility.** Taking responsibility means being accountable and taking ownership of your actions. It means accepting the consequences of your decisions, good or bad, and learning from them. In order to take responsibility, it is important to think carefully about your decisions, be honest with yourself and others, and actively seek out solutions to any problems that arise. It is also important to be transparent and admit when you make mistakes, while also taking steps to ensure they are not repeated.

5. **Seek Understanding.** Seeking understanding involves asking questions, listening and engaging in meaningful conversations, and seeking out different perspectives. It is important to be open-minded and patient when discussing sensitive topics with others, as this allows for deeper discussion and improved comprehension. Researching the topic can also help provide insight and increased understanding.

6. **Respect Others.** To respect others, it is important to treat them with kindness and consideration, listen to their ideas with an open mind, and value their feelings and opinions. It also means respecting their boundaries and respecting

their right to privacy. Additionally, it is important to give them the benefit of the doubt and remain open-minded without judging them in any way.

7. **Be Humble.** Being humble means having an accurate view of yourself, knowing your strengths and weaknesses, and having a willingness to learn from those around you. It also means being open to feedback and criticism, and not feeling the need to compare yourself to others. It means appreciating the accomplishments of others and not feeling threatened by their successes. Finally, maintaining a sense of humility involves not bragging or boasting about yourself and your accomplishments.

8. **Practice Patience.** Practicing patience includes understanding that delays and difficulties are a part of life, that it is important to accept these experiences without complaining. Understand that complaining rarely changes the situation that is causing your frustration. Consider taking a few deep breaths and focusing on the things you can accomplish in this moment. Whenever you feel stuck in the present, focus your thoughts on planning a future goal, activity, or adventure. You can also consider putting on your favorite music, listening to an inspirational speaker, or other learning activity.

9. **Show Gratitude.** Gratitude is a feeling of appreciation or thanks for something that someone has done for you. It is a recognition that they have deliberately chose to serve or support you. Your gratitude can be expressed through

your words or actions. Many people find that writing in a gratitude journal helps them keep focused on all the blessings they have, even when there are specific things lacking in their lives.

10. **Cultivate Contentment.** Contentment is a state of happiness and satisfaction with one's circumstances. It is an understanding that life is good despite its imperfections, and that it can be enjoyed without the need for more. Contentment can be cultivated by simply being in the present moment, noticing the people and beauty around you, and savoring these small moments of joy. It also involves learning to accept situations that we can't change or control. Finally, it includes engaging in activities that bring joy and fulfillment, such as spending quality time with loved ones, dedicating time to hobbies and interests, and simply slowing down and taking a break when needed.

11. **Show Kindness.** Being kind starts with the way we speak and interact with others. Being patient and understanding, generous with honest compliments, offering to help someone in need, or lending a friendly ear are all simple acts of kindness. Using your time, resources, and energy helping those in need are also powerful acts of kindness and compassion.

12. **Persevere Through Adversity.** Persevering through adversity involves having a resilient mindset and focusing on the positive aspects of the situation. It also involves setting realistic goals and taking consistent small steps to

achieve them. Having a support system of friends, family, and professionals is essential in helping you stay motivated and encouraged when facing difficulties. Finally, having a healthy lifestyle with adequate sleep, exercise, and proper nutrition will help you have the energy to stay focused on your goals during tough times.

13. **Pursue Justice.** We must be willing to stand up for our rights, the rights of others, and challenge any form of injustice or inequality that we encounter. We must support laws that ensure that everyone is treated equally and that they are applied consistently.

14. **Seek Harmony.** It is important to respect individual differences and find balance between conflicting interests, opinions, and beliefs. By listening to each other's perspectives and communicating openly, we can create an atmosphere of trust and understanding, which will help reconcile differences, allow us to find common ground for collaboration and compromise, and achieve harmony.

15. **Develop Self Awareness.** Self-awareness is the process of gaining an understanding of our feelings, thoughts, motivations, and behaviors. To become more self-aware, we can practice self-reflection, observe how we respond in different situations, engage in positive self-talk, recognize our strengths, and take time to understand ourselves in relation to others. We can pay attention to how our thoughts and emotions affect our behavior, and then better manage our reactions.

16. **Live With Balance.** Living with balance is all about finding the right combination of activities, rest, and healthy lifestyle choices that allow us to feel fulfilled, manage our stress levels, avoid burnout, and stay healthy. This includes eating a balanced diet, getting sufficient exercise, getting enough sleep and rest, setting aside time for yourself and your personal interests, managing your workload, and connecting with others in meaningful ways.

17. **Practice Compassion.** Practicing compassion starts with cultivating a nonjudgmental mindset and being kind and understanding to others. Remember that everyone is on their own journey and that each situation is unique. Learn to communicate with empathy and actively seek out opportunities to show kindness, understanding, and gratitude. Approach difficult conversations with the goal of understanding the other person's perspective and find compassion for them even if you do not agree with their views. Be willing to forgive yourself and others for mistakes and always look for the good in people and situations.

18. **Respect Our Elders.** This is a reminder to show appreciation and admiration for those who have lived longer and have had more life experiences than you. It means to treat them with kindness, understanding, and recognition of their experience and wisdom.

19. **Share Joy and Laughter.** Studies have shown that joy and laughter help our bodies heal from accidents or surgeries quicker. As the saying goes, "laughter is the best medicine." Our fondest memories are often anchored to feelings of joy. Share both generously.

20. **Enjoy Healthy Humor.** Humor can help us keep our perspective during trying times. It can lighten the mood when there are tensions in the room. It can take heavy feelings and offset them with lighter thoughts. Pointing out the irony of a situation can make even a tough challenge funny.

21. **Serve with Love.** This means to serve others with kindness, compassion, and an open heart. It is about putting the needs of others before your own and doing so in a way that shows genuine care and concern. Serving with love is about understanding that even small acts of kindness can have a big impact on those around us. Love is one of the few things that the more you give, the more you get back. Love is about abundance, and there is no limit to its reach.

> **❝** I believe that when we are judged by our Creator, it will be based on how well we developed and applied these principles in our lives.

Applying these principles in our lives will help us develop and strengthen our personal character traits and increase our capacity to contribute to society by loving and serving others. I believe that when we are judged by our Creator, it will be based on how well we developed and applied these principles in our lives.

We have been given a unique gift that no other living creatures possess—the ability to step outside of ourselves (figuratively speaking) and reflect on our own thinking and behavior. This gives us the opportunity to consider situations that we may encounter in the future and commit to responding in a way that is aligned with these correct principles.

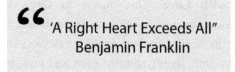

" 'A Right Heart Exceeds All"
Benjamin Franklin

Steven Covey taught us that our personal choice lies in that moment between stimulus and response. When we react impulsively to something that happens to us, we often make decisions that we are not proud of later. By giving ourselves a moment to think we can then choose our response more deliberately, we can ensure that our responses and actions are aligned with the character traits we wish to emulate. By considering potential situations in advance, we can pre-determine our response. This allows us to shorten the time needed in the moment of choice so that we can respond both timely and effectively. This is a powerful ability that we can all develop.

Benjamin Franklin is famous for applying his list of thirteen virtues throughout his life in his autobiography. He would practice each one daily for a week, reflect on his progress, and then continue to the next one, continuing the rotation through all the virtues. It is said that his friend recommended the thirteenth virtue of humility to him, but he often felt so good about his progress on the first twelve that he had a hard time with humility! Talking about virtue, Benjamin Franklin said, "A Right Heart Exceeds All."

By regularly working on our own personal development, we can increase our capacity to live these key principles throughout our lives and become an example to those around us. There is much that has been said and written to guide our efforts. But at the end of the day, we must align our efforts with the values and principles that we believe in; otherwise, we will not be motivated to action.

Brendon Burchard makes several key points about how to get and stay motivated.

1. Motive is the root word which means ... reason for action.
2. The mother of motivation is choice. We think about a situation then make a choice to act or not. Our clarity and commitment to the choice determine our motivation.
3. If we want more motivation in our lives, we must make clearer choices and be more deeply committed to them. It is that simple.
4. Motivation is sparked by the energy created by ambition and expectancy.
5. Ambition is the choice to be, have, do, or experience something greater in our lives. As soon as we want

something greater for ourselves, our motivation is sparked.

6. Expectancy means that we believe we can make it happen, or we will not even try. Expectancy is the difference between hope and motivation.

7. You sustain motivation through attention and effort. The deeper and longer your attention and effort, the more motivation you feel.

8. We must focus relentlessly on our ambitions and act decisively toward them.

9. We must continue our efforts and attention to our ambitions despite fatigue, distractions, and hardship.

10. Attitude matters. Free and motivated people are positive and enthusiastic toward their goals and their lives.

11. We must be vigilant and surround ourselves with genuine and positive people.

12. We must spark our souls with an ambitious fire. Stoke our energy with close attention, constant effort, and positive attitude.

This is good council. By aligning our actions with our core values, we will find it much easier to stay motivated.

Michael Saylor gives us this advice on his top ten values:

1. Focus your energy.
2. Guard your time.
3. Train your mind.
4. Train your body.
5. Think for yourself.
6. Curate your friends.
7. Curate your environment.

8. Keep your promises.
9. Stay cheerful and constructive.
10. Upgrade the world.

Michael is a brilliant and kind billionaire. He has run a successful public company for thirty years; a company he formed right after graduating from MIT. He is a leading Bitcoin spokesperson and influencer. He provides free conferences for businesses that want to adopt Bitcoin as their treasury reserves, and he offers all the tools and resources they need to implement.

He has created an organization, Saylor.org, that provides free college courses that are fully accredited where students can earn full degrees. He has 1,530,841 students who have started their journey. He believes a college education should be free for all who are willing to put in the time and effort.

He lives his value to upgrade the world in all that he does. He is a good man. He is an example to all of us. He would probably be embarrassed by my praise.

As we think about the world we want to leave our grandchildren, we should take some time to reflect on what we believe, the values we hold, and the nonnegotiable principles that we are committed to teach and live. Aligning our actions with our values generates the motivation and courage we need to push forward. Good men and women, fortified with correct principles and committed to living them, are a powerful force to be reckoned with. Each of us can, and should, work to improve ourselves and emulate correct principles in our lives, be good examples to others, and show them that we don't need to take advantage of others to be successful.

> **"** Good men and women,
> fortified with correct
> principles and committed
> to living them, are a
> powerful force to be
> reckoned with.

What good can we do if we apply our energy and passion to this effort? Think of the influence we can have on the next generation as they see our lives aligned with these values. They will be motivated to emulate our behaviors in their lives and, in so doing, prepare them to lead the generation after them.

This is the power of correct principles. They stand the test of time. They stabilize families, communities, and nations who adhere to them. They encourage us to do good. They encourage us to be good. They are aligned with our innate sense of right and wrong. They help each of us transition over the course of our lives from our naturally selfish beginnings to selfless lives of compassion and service. These are eternal principles that ring true in our souls, and we know they are right. To go against these principles is to ignore what is noble and good about humanity.

Correct Principles are the mortar that holds society together.

Therefore, We Shall Teach Correct Principles.

"These are eternal principles that ring true in our souls, and we know they are right.

We Shall Teach Correct Principles
Challenge

1. Take the 21 Principles Personal Assessment at the back of the book.
2. List three that you feel you practice consistently in your daily life.
3. For each of these, list an example or describe how you have applied the principle.
4. Teach one of these principles to your child or grandchild.
5. List three that you aspire to practice in your daily life.
6. For each of your aspirations, list an example of someone you look up to who lives that principle in their daily lives.
7. Develop a personal development plan to implement your aspirational practices.
8. Write a statement for each of your aspirational principles, describing them as if you have mastered them in your life.

WE SHALL STRENGTHEN OUR FAMILIES

Families are the smallest unit in a functioning society. They are the critical glue that holds everything else together. Families are where we feel loved and supported, learn correct principles, learn to share and get along with others, and learn the value of work, personal contribution, and service.

The work of parenting is hard. Life is a journey from selfishness to selflessness, and those little ones who we are teaching these principles to all start at the selfish end of the spectrum. They often don't understand or appreciate our efforts until many years later, usually after they become parents!

The true joy of being a grandparent is watching your children raise your grandchildren. This is when you will know if your efforts were successful. Of course, we are always a little concerned that they will mess up our grandkids! But this is the circle of life—the passing of the torch to the next generation.

Families are the building blocks of society and are critical for a strong foundation. If families are the building blocks, then correct principles are the mortar that hold the blocks together. Together, they help us form social structures, such as businesses, schools, and government organizations, that serve our communities, states, nations, and the world at large. As any good architect or engineer knows, a weak foundation can crack and break and bring the whole building down.

Satan and his globalist minions have worked tirelessly to weaken our families, destroy correct principles, and bring down society. They have accomplished this by devaluing and demeaning the fathers of our families. Getting them addicted to drugs and alcohol, tempting them with lusts of the flesh, and destroying their confidence are just some of the tools that Satan uses to leave them feeling useless and hopeless.

This leaves the mothers to fend for themselves and their children in a dark and often scary world. Trying to be both the provider and nurturer often leaves our mothers exhausted and ineffective at parenting.

Children are regularly left alone for long periods and don't get the support they need to succeed in school or to have appropriate social opportunities for their development. It is not surprising that most crimes are committed by the children of single parent families.

> **"** God designed the family to have a mother and a father who work together in partnership to create an environment where children can experience love and support.

This is not God's way. God designed the family to have a mother and a father who work together in partnership to create an environment where children can experience love and support, where parents teach by example correct principles. In this environment, children can make small mistakes, be lovingly corrected, and develop strong moral character. In this environment, children can learn to work together with their parents to experience the joy of accomplishment, the joy of serving others, and the joy of building trust and creating lifelong relationships.

When we, as parents, model these behaviors, our children learn how to emulate them in their own lives. The goal of parenting is to produce honest, hard-working adults with a desire to serve and contribute to the well-being of others. Parenting is hard. Parenting is critical. Good parenting is the basis for strong societies.

> **❝** Parenting is hard. Parenting is critical. Good parenting is the basis for strong societies.

Children need rules. Children need boundaries. When you first take them bowling, you start them out with bumper rails to ensure that their ball stays in the lane, avoiding the failure of a gutter ball. Once they develop more skill, you can remove the rails and they are successful staying in the lane without the bumpers. Boundaries serve a similar role to keep their behavior within reasonable parameters until they learn to make good decisions on their own.

Big mistakes early in their lives can thus be avoided. Not knowing how to cross the road, swim in a pool, or manage a hot stove can be devastating to the uneducated child when first encountering these situations in life. However, our role as parents is not to train them to live in fear, but to teach them a healthy respect for the dangers of life and give them the courage to try new things and expand their skills and accomplishments.

Think back to when you first learned how to ride a bike. It felt like there was so much to do at one time! You had to pedal, balance, steer, and navigate all at the same time. But once you got the hang of it, the newfound freedom was amazing! You could feel the wind on your face, lean into the corners, jump the curbs, brake on a dime! Your world expanded as you could now travel greater distances with ease and experience new adventures.

Guess what? Your parents likely taught you to ride. They were right there behind you in those wobbly moments, holding the seat and running alongside you. They only let go when they thought you were sufficiently skilled to do it on your own. As you rode away, they stood there behind you, both proud of you and a little scared for you. But they knew you needed to become self-sufficient at this new skill.

There is a joy in parenting that you don't feel with other successes in life. Parents have an innate desire to see their children succeed in all that they do, and when their children exceed their own skills in any given area, the parent is not jealous but grateful that they were able to provide the support that allowed their child to excel.

Likewise, when a child is suffering due to an illness or accident, parents would rather take on the pain themselves if it meant sparing their children. This is the love a parent has for their child. This is a love that is hard for a parent to explain to an adult without children. This love of a parent gives us a small taste of the love that God has for each of us. It is amazing that He has given us the gift of procreation to allow us to experience this level of love in our lives!

> **" Strengthening our families starts with strengthening our marriages.**

Strengthening our families starts with strengthening our marriages. If the parents' relationship is on rocky ground, it is hard to give the needed attention to the children.

Every close relationship is based on trust. To earn another's trust, you must be trustworthy. This means you must consistently show by your actions that you are reliable, honest, truthful, and act in an ethical manner. In an intimate relationship, it also means you are loyal and committed to the relationship for the long term. You must be in tune with your partner's emotional sensitivities and needs. You must have open lines of communication and be willing to listen and be supportive. If you focus on what you can give to the relationship and not what you expect your partner to give, you will find that your love and attention are most often reciprocated by your partner.

Because we all have agency to make our own choices, we cannot coerce another in our intimate relationships. We must influence with love and compassion. Like all organic things in life, the love we have for our partners is either growing or, through neglect, starting to wither. Therefore, we must never take our relationships for granted but continually nourish them to keep them strong.

Setting aside regular time together, away from the children, is good for all. Parents get intimate quiet time and children learn to be independent in these breaks from their parents. Parents who give all their time and attention to their children at the exclusion of taking care of themselves or their partners often get burned out and feel like they have lost themselves. This is not heathy for the parent and, over time, not healthy for the child, either. As in all things, balance is the key to happiness and success.

When children see their parents love and respect each other, they learn how to practice this in their own relationships. This is particularly important when the parents have divorced.

Too often, basic civility suffers. Parents in this situation must realize that they will be co-parenting their children and grandchildren for the rest of their lives, and their children will certainly notice how they treat each other. When children see parents working through challenges together, settling differences in a fair and loving way and always focusing on a commitment to the family, they begin to understand the important role that families play in society.

> **"** When children see that their parents love and respect each other, they learn how to practice this in their own relationships.

Extended families often provide critical support for individual families. Parents, grandparents, siblings, aunts, uncles, and cousins can all play an important role in the success of an individual family. They can give advice and support in many ways.

I once spoke with an Indian woman, who had an arranged marriage, about her thoughts on choosing her own mate or having one chosen for her. I was impressed by her answer. She said that, in an arranged marriage, both families have a vested interest in the success of the marriage and work together to ensure the couple start off on a solid foundation. She said that they are all committed to the marriage and help overcome challenges and obstacles along the way. She said she believed that the reason we have so many divorces in America is because couples do not have that same level of support.

While I personally choose to exercise my agency when selecting a spouse, I find her point about the extra family support to be valid. Too often, we lack this deep commitment to our marriages and, at the slightest trouble, we abandon the hope and promise we felt in the beginning. Extended family support can be what we need to keep our marriages intact through the challenges that inevitably appear.

Friends can also be a great support to families. While there are toxic relationships that should be dissolved, most marriages can be saved. Friends are often the ones who we go to for advice on these matters.

As a friend giving advice on matters of the heart, we should be cautious that we don't tell them what they want to hear (i.e., you deserve better, you don't need to put up with that behavior, you are a victim, you should leave them, you are better off on your own). While these things may be true, a good friend would also give balanced advice and encourage them to try to save their marriage.

We might ask them what behaviors they exhibit that may make their spouse feel underappreciated, unloved, or unimportant. We might ask them why they were attracted to their spouse and how they felt in the beginning of the relationship. We might ask them what the top five traits are that they love about their spouse. We might ask them what they could do for their spouse to help them feel more loved. We might ask them what they could do to add vibrancy and passion back to the relationship.

Most people are waiting for their spouse to make the first move to improve the relationship, but that takes away one's personal power to act. By helping your friend focus on the things that they can do, you can help them take personal responsibility for their half of the relationship. In the end, both parties have shared responsibility for the success or failure of their relationship.

Divorce is messy, and many of the implications are not fully understood until it is too late. Don't encourage them to abandon this critical intimate relationship over issues that can be resolved and don't encourage them to give up without a fight.

Once they give up on their first marriage, their commitment to future relationships can also suffer. Thoughts like, "I wouldn't put up with this before, I am certainly not going to put up with this now," or "I promised myself I would never do this again," can weaken their resolve to deal with any challenges in the future. I really think this is why so many second or third marriages don't pass the test of time or last as long as the first marriage. As their friend, we should help them strengthen and fortify their current relationships, if possible.

When I was twelve, I went to work at a bicycle shop. The owner was in his late sixties and had never been married. I worked there full-time in the summer and part-time during the school year for six years. I learned a lot from him. I learned to spoke a wheel, straighten and weld a frame, tune gears and brakes, and rebuild bicycle transmissions. I learned to sell and handle customer service issues. I learned how to make copies of keys and program locks. I learned how to run a cash register and order supplies and inventory, and deal with vendors.

But the main lesson I learned from George Carlson was that this life was not meant to be lived alone! I saw firsthand how little love he had in his life and what a small sad existence he experienced. He lived in the back of the store, had little family, and was not part of any social groups or organized religion. He had no hobbies or close friends. He became an alcoholic and eventually died a lonely death. I knew right then that I wanted a family of my own.

My father came from a broken home. When he was fourteen, he and his father jumped a train and traveled from California to Montana to start a new life. He tells how they sat on an open train car, in the bucket of a front-end loader, and soaked up the sunshine. It seemed like a grand adventure awaited them. Later, as it got cold and miserable, he began to question the decision.

Once in Montana, his father got a job as a ranch hand, and they tended sheep. It wasn't long before his father, who was an alcoholic, started on his drinking binges and abandoned my father.

At age fifteen, my father found himself alone in Montana with no friends or relatives, or support of any kind. He would stay in jails just to have a warm place to sleep. He enrolled himself at a local high school and asked the gym teacher if he might live with them for a while. The gym teacher agreed and offered him their attic.

The gym teacher had a family and would always invite my father to join them for dinner and activities. My dad never wanted to impose and often would just look down from the attic, wishing and dreaming about having a family of his own. It breaks my heart to think of the pain he felt.

Now he is the father of five, grandfather of sixteen, great-grandfather of twenty-seven, and great-great-grandfather of one. I would say that his dream came true! Having lived without a real family, he understood the importance of one.

Families are where correct principles are taught, and families are the building blocks of a healthy society.

Therefore, We Shall Strengthen Our Families.

WE SHALL STRENGTHEN OUR FAMILIES CHALLENGE

1. Complete the Family Assessment at the back of the book.
2. Have your spouse or partner complete the assessment.
3. Compare notes and write your top three strengths as a family unit.
4. Describe the top three challenges that you struggle with.
5. Develop a family creed, detailing a minimum of five statements that you both commit to adhere to as members of the family.
6. Share this with your children and get their input and commitment. Tweak as needed to get their buy-in.
7. Post your family creed in a visible location that all family members see on a regular basis.
8. When you have a success or challenge in your family, refer to your creed and your commitment to live it.

WE SHALL SERVE IN OUR COMMUNITIES

While families are the core unit of society, communities are the structure where our families and businesses can expand our influence for good in the world. Communities are where we expand application of the correct principles we have been taught.

Will we be honest in our dealings with others? Will we show compassion when others stumble? Will we step up when we see someone in need? Will we deliver on our promises? Will we counsel and teach the uneducated? Will we give fair value for other's labor? Will we honor our mentors by mentoring others?

Every day, we will have opportunities to exercise our agency in these areas and more. Community is where we can apply the skills that we have developed to help make the world a better place.

> **"**Community is where we can apply the skills we have developed to help make the world a better place.

Service can be offered in many ways, from formal programs to spontaneous acts. Serving in our communities is a vital part of being a member of society. It is an act of kindness and compassion, and it can have a profound impact on people's lives, both in the short-term and in the long-term.

There are many ways we can serve in our communities and bless the lives of others. In my own local neighborhood, there are seventeen aging widows. I am always impressed to see good families helping them by tending to their yards, doing their grocery shopping, shoveling their snow, and picking them up to take them to church or to doctor appointments.

One sweet old widow is becoming hard of hearing and cannot hear the speakers at church, so one of my good friends found an electronic mic that he helps place in her ear each Sunday so that she can hear the sermon. What a sweet act of compassion and service.

Another way to serve in our communities is through volunteer work. Any spare time you have can be put to good use by using it to help in your local community. Whether it is collecting donations for a charity or volunteering at a homeless shelter, all acts of service, no matter how small, will make a positive change in the lives of those around you.

Additionally, volunteering for causes that concern you and align with your values can be incredibly meaningful and rewarding.

> **❝** Volunteering for causes that concern you and align with your values can be incredibly meaningful and rewarding.

We can also serve in our communities by taking part in organizational activities or initiatives. Participating in campaigns, events, and programs put on by local organizations can bring about lasting positive changes in our communities. Not only do these projects help improve our communities, but they are also a great way to build relationships with others in our communities. Working side by side gives us an opportunity to create genuine and lasting relationships.

We have organized our community to be prepared for potential natural disasters. We have block captains assigned to every ten families. These block captains have handheld radios. Monthly radio checks are performed where the block captains check in with neighborhood leaders who then check in with city leaders who manage emergency response teams and resources.

Each family is given two laminated 8x11 cards. One has an "*OK*" symbol and the other has a "*Need Help*" symbol. In an emergency, the family can post this in the window or hang it on their door to give the block captains a quick visual indicator of their current status. It also informs the block captain and directs their efforts to determine what is needed so they can communicate up to the emergency response teams. This is a good example of the strength that can exist in a cohesive community.

In a recent weather event, we experienced 110 mile per hour winds. Roofs were damaged, trees and fences were knocked down, power was interrupted. Neighbors responded quickly with teams going from house to house, cutting up the trees and hauling off the debris. Every night for a full week, neighbors showed up to help each other. Trucks and trailers and chainsaws were everywhere. Many friendships were formed as we worked side by side.

One neighbor said in jest that we needed another disaster. What he was really saying was that he looked forward to the next opportunity to work and serve together.

The women in our neighborhood have also organized around helping families with new babies by bringing in meals and helping with household duties. One good neighbor even helped deliver a baby when the mid-wife was unable to arrive in time for the scheduled home delivery. They also bring meals to families that are sick or where family members have had recent surgeries. In addition, they support families who have lost loved ones by hosting luncheons after the funeral to ease the burden on the family during those trying times.

Mentoring is another great way to serve in our communities and bless the lives of others. Providing guidance and assistance in education to those around us gives us the opportunity to help others develop their own self-confidence and skills.

Apprenticeship programs have long been an effective way to transfers skills to the next generation through formal mentoring programs. The apprentice can learn and master skills by actively participating in on-the-job training. Most skills take about five years to master, at which time they are competent to provide quality products or services to the community. The mentor also benefits from the relationship, as they get satisfaction from teaching and watching their protégés succeed. We need to reestablish more apprenticeship opportunities across our industry and service sectors.

Formal roles in our communities are another important way to serve. Local churches and governments can provide opportunities for assignments or projects.

One of my neighbors is the mayor of our little town. Although he has another full-time job, he spends a lot of time handling issues in our town and providing leadership to our community. He is a good man, and I am grateful for his service.

Another neighbor serves an important role as a key religious leader responsible for a group of 4,500 members of our church. He leads and guides efforts to strengthen our families and youth. Programs are available to help with any struggles that families may be having from financial issues, health issues, marital issues, or substance abuse issues. He does this work without monetary compensation.

Others serve at our local prison, bringing messages of hope and redemption to the inmates. Hundreds of others in our community serve in various capacities, as well, donating their time and talents to serve any in need.

Historically, villages and small towns have served as our core communities, providing service and support for all the members. Everyone knew each other and contributed to the success of the community. In many cases, they had to combine efforts and share duties to provide for their joint needs. Fire departments were often composed of volunteers, neighbors helped each other build barns and harvest crops. Posses were formed from the community to assist the sheriff in pursuing criminals. These shared roles were born of necessity as the communities were often remote and outside help was not available on demand.

In modern society, we have become accustomed to getting nearly anything we need with a phone call—police, fire, plumber, ambulance, etc. These services are convenient but, as a result, we have become less self-sufficient and more dependent on these professionals.

A hundred years ago, a typical farming/ranching family could grow their own food and raise animals for meat, eggs, milk, and cheese. They could sew their own clothes, build their own homes, repair tools, and provide for the basic necessities. Today, these skills are rarely found in our families and communities. This leaves us vulnerable to disruptions in our modern supply chains.

The average grocery store has two days of inventory. When a catastrophe happens, stores are stripped bare in hours as people rush to buy needed supplies. This is where we need to be more resilient in our families and communities.

> **"When a catastrophe happens, stores are stripped bare in hours, as people rush to buy needed supplies. This is where we need to be more resilient in our families**

By preparing for your own family's needs, with extra to spare, you are serving your community in two ways. First, you will not be a burden to the community when disaster strikes. Secondly, you will have spare supplies to help support others in your community who were not as prepared or who suffered losses due to the catastrophe. Each of us has a duty and an obligation to be as self-sufficient as we can become.

Recall the popular children's story of the grasshoppers and the ants made popular in the Pixar movie *A Bug's Life*.

The ants worked and prepared while it was warm and the sun shined. The grasshoppers played and relaxed and were ill-prepared when the weather turned against them, and then they became a burden as they demanded that the ants support them.

In every catastrophe that befalls humans, you find those who follow the pattern of the ants and those who are more like the grasshoppers. The time to prepare is clearly before the catastrophe hits while the sun is still shining.

It is much better to be part of the solution than adding to the problem that increases the burden others must bear.

We have seen this many times with self-inflicted emergencies where a hiker goes into the woods ill-prepared, has an accident, or succumbs to foul weather. Then search and rescue must drop what they are doing and expend time and resources, often risking their own lives to save the culprit who could have easily avoided the situation through better preparation.

We owe it to those around us to not become a burden to our families or communities due to our poor choices. Better to be able to support and serve when needed.

> **"** Strong communities create safety and support for all members. We all need to be a part of a community.

In summary, there are many ways to serve in our communities. From small spontaneous acts to taking on formal roles and responsibilities, we can all find ways to serve if we are willing. My hope is that these examples motivate others to serve in their communities.

Communities are important. Strong communities create safety and support for all members. We all need to be a part of a community. In our communities, we have an opportunity to expand our circle of influence for good.

Therefore, We Shall Serve in Our Communities.

WE SHALL SERVE IN OUR COMMUNITIES CHALLENGE

1. List five examples of community service you have rendered in the past. These can be formal roles or informal acts of service.
2. List three ideas for community service that you and your family could do together. Target two to four hours.
3. Commit and schedule to do one of these projects in the next thirty days.

WE SHALL REBUILD OUR ECONOMIES

Small businesses are the true engine of the economy. Entrepreneurs and Engineers are the innovators. They produce more jobs than any other sector and over half of the innovations that we enjoy.

The attack on small businesses was a deliberate act by the globalists to destroy the middle class. We must understand that the globalists want two distinct classes of people—the Global Elite (self-proclaimed) and a slave class who they control and who does all the work for them. They cannot tolerate an independent middle class of thriving small businesses.

> **"** Small businesses are the true engine of the economy. Entrepreneurs and Engineers are the innovators.

It is not surprising that, during the recent "Covid pandemic," they deemed the large global businesses that they control to be "Essential," while discounting all small businesses as "non-Essential."

The arrogance of this position is striking! Who are they to decide which of us should be allowed to enjoy economic freedom and make a living to feed our families and pursue our dreams? Our Founding Fathers clearly recognized this when they stated in the Declaration of Independence: "We hold these truths to be self-evident, that all men are created equal, that they are endowed by their Creator with certain unalienable Rights, that among these are Life, Liberty, and the pursuit of Happiness." This could not be clearer!

Creating a business that serves the community is a practical solution. By bringing together capital, people, and ideas, we can create a valuable service that is needed in the community. Both the customer and the owner benefit. The customer receives the product or service, and the owner provides for their family.

There are so many options for products and services that everyone can find something they enjoy, that the world needs, and is willing to pay for.

> **"** Everyone can find something they enjoy, that the world needs, and is willing to pay for.

Robert Kiyosaki is famous for his *Rich Dad Poor Dad* series, including the *Cashflow Quadrant* where he teaches in practical terms the different employment models that we can choose from.

There are four main choices:

1. **Employee:** working for someone else.
2. **Self-Employed:** where you own a job.
3. **Business:** where you have employees working for you.

4. **Investor:** where your money works for you.

As you consider your current skill set, you can map it onto these options to see which is the best fit for you.

To begin rebuilding our economies we must have more control over our work than we would normally have as an employee. Additionally, many large employers are owned by the global elite that are crushing small businesses, so we do not want to support them if possible. This means that the two best options will be self-employed or business.

The key difference between the two can be determined by a simple test. If you take time off, does the business continue to operate? If you are self-employed, you are likely wearing many hats in your business (i.e., marketing, sales, operations, finance, etc.). When you are not working there is no one else to handle these items and nothing gets done. You own a job.

There are many professional services that fall into this category, like doctors and attorneys who are not working directly for a larger firm. There are also many service and construction businesses that fall into this category. Many of these businesses can provide a good living and can be started with little capital.

> **"** Many of these businesses can provide a good living and can be started with little capital.

The main drawbacks are:

1. They are dependent on your labor to generate revenue.
2. You are constantly balancing selling versus delivering your product or service.
3. They are hard to sell to when you want to retire because they are totally dependent on your skill set to operate.

However, even with these drawbacks, they are easy to set up, can be started as a side project, and then be grown into a business over time.

Product or Service?

You can sell a service.

The advantage here is you are selling primarily labor, starting with you. This can generate a revenue stream quickly. Good consultants can bill about 50% of their time, as the remaining 50% is spent selling the service and managing the business. If you can bill your time at $250 per hour, this results in revenue of $250k per year (2000 hours x 50% x $250). If you can only sell your time for $100 per hour, you can expect revenue around 100k per year. High-end consultants can bill out at $500 to $750 per hour but, at that level, you likely need employees to help you run the business.

When you are selling labor, you generally can mark up your costs by 100%. So, if your employee's salary is 80k, you would add about 25% for payroll taxes and benefits. This would bring your cost to 100k. You would multiply your cost times two to calculate the revenue the employee must generate, or 200k in revenue. Then you must calculate the percentage of the employee's time that will be billable. It is not reasonable that they will be 100% efficient, but because they are either delivering the service or selling the service (usually not both), they will be more efficient than you when you are trying to fill both roles. But they will have setup time, training time, and vacation and holiday time.

Billable Rates	
Total Available Hours	2000
Billable Percentage	50%
Billable Hours	1000
Billable Rate Per Hour	$250
Total Annual Revenue	$250,000
Calculating Employee Billable Rates	
Employee Salary	$80,000
Payroll Taxes and Benefits%	25%
Payroll Taxes and Benefits	$20,000
Total Cost per Employee	$100,000
Markup %	100%
Total Revenue Per Employee	$200,000
Total Hours Available	2000
Billable %	65%
Total Billable Hours	1335
Hourly Billable Rate	$150

Let's be conservative and assume they will be billable 65% of the time. Taking 2,000 hours per year x 65% gives us 1,335 hours billable hours. So, to generate 200k in revenue, we will need to price our hourly billing rate at $150 per hour

($200,000 / 1,335 = $150). Not surprisingly, this is a typical shop rate for auto mechanics and other labor-intensive professional services.

> **"** If you want to scale the business to a level you can manage the business without selling or delivering the service, then you will need around 20 employees.

If you want to scale the business to a level you can manage the business without selling or delivering the service, then you will need around 20 employees, as a rule of thumb. Many businessowners struggle when they have 5 to 10 employees because, at that level, they need to manage the team and still sell or deliver the service part of the time. This is a real challenge and causes a lot of owners to burn out.

The other challenge is that the owner is usually an expert in delivering the service but has little experience teaching and managing others. An owner's common compliant at this phase is that no one can deliver the service like they can, or provide the great customer service that they deliver, but they don't know how to upskill their employees to get past this hurdle. This is because they have not built out systems and processes that help insure their employees can deliver a consistent product. The 80/20 rule applies here. 80% of issues can be traced back to deficient systems or processes, with only 20% due to employee error.

Finances also can be a challenge. Continuing with our example, let's assume that you have five employees generating 200k each in revenue. This means you have 1M in annual revenue. Your cost would include their labor at $500k, plus estimated overhead of 25% or 250k. This leaves you with 250k for you as the owner. If you paid yourself the same 250k, you could have billed as a one-person shop that would leave you with zero profit for you as the owner/investor. This is not good—a 0% net profit on 1M in sales. No real return for the extra risk and hassle of managing another five people every day and dealing with all their personal issues. Oh yes, there will be personal issues!

Profitability	5 Employees	20 Employees
Number of Employees	5	20
Revenue Per Employee	$200,000	$200,000
Total Revenue	$1,000,000	$4,000,000
Labor Percentage	50%	50%
Direct Labor Costs	$500,000	$2,000,000
Number of Managers	0	2
Cost Per Manager	$0	$125,000
Management Salaries	$0	$250,000
Other Overhead %	25%	25%
Other Overhead Costs	$250,000	$1,000,000
Total Overhead	$250,000	$1,250,000
Profit Before Owner Salary	$250,000	$750,000
Owners Salary	$250,000	$250,000
Net Profit	$0	$500,000
Net Profit %	0.00%	12.50%

> **"** Free up your time to work on the business building systems and processes that will generate efficiencies and higher bottom line profits.

However, if you can quickly scale to 20 or more employees, you can get through this awkward stage, have the revenue to hire 2 managers who can manage 10 employees each, and free up your time to work on the business building systems and processes that will generate efficiencies and higher bottom line profits.

Continuing the example, if you have 20 employees generating 200k each in revenue, your business will generate 4M per year. Now the math makes more sense. 2M in labor costs with 2 managers at $125k each and 25% overhead of 1M leaves you 750k before paying your salary. If you pay yourself the same base of 250k, you now have 500k in profit for you as the owner. This is around 12.5% profit, a decent return for many businesses. But it is 300% of what you were making with 5 employees. The lesson is either stay small with low risk or have a plan to scale quickly to a level that gets you past the awkward stage, with profits that justify the extra complexity and risk.

You can sell a physical product.

Most markets are highly competitive, and it can be challenging to get a high markup on your product. Most products have a 5 to 40% markup on your cost. For our example, we will use 25%. If the product costs you $100 and you mark it up 25%, most people think you have a 25% profit. However, this is not the case. If you mark it up 25%, your sales price would be $125. But your actual profit is only 20%, calculated as follows $125 - $100 = $25 dollar profit. But $25 is only 20% of the sales price $25 / $125 = 20%. This often confuses new owners and businesspeople. That may not seem significant, but when most businesses operate on thin profit margins of 5% or less, it is the difference between making a profit and only breaking even after all your hard work.

Inventory and supply chain management are additional complications when selling a physical product. There is a delicate balance between these. Efficient supply chain management dictates that you keep little inventory and deliver the product on demand. While some products, like books, can be printed one at a time as needed, many products require more time to manufacture and deliver.

Inventory acts as the buffer to ensure you have product to sell in the event of a disruption in your supply chain. The problem is that inventory is expensive to store, often requires the seller to purchase from their supplier before they have an actual sale, and the products can be stolen or damaged and therefore must be insured, incurring additional costs. You might also have losses due to theft of your inventory.

You can sell software as a service.

The beauty of software is the scalability it offers. Once you create the software, selling a license to the next customer can be done for a small incremental cost. It is not unreasonable to generate 1 to 2 million in revenue per employee compared to the $200k in our earlier example. Also, most software companies can generate profits in the 30 to 40% range, which is significantly higher than the previous examples. However, there are drawbacks to this model.

Because of the demand for software developers, you will be paying a much higher cost per employee. Software developers also tend to move from company to company for a higher salary and/or more varied experience. As a result, they don't have a lot of loyalty. This can be disruptive to your organizational knowledge base as you are constantly retraining your team.

Another challenge is that software is never complete and, as tools and methods progress, you will have a need to rebuild the software several times over the product's lifetime. The cost to host your software service is also significant. You can host with a cloud service that is scalable, but also expensive, or you can host it in a colocation data center where you lease space in a rack that comes with redundant power and internet services, but you need to provide the hardware that runs your actual application. This is usually a lower cost than a full cloud solution, but your hardware will only last 3 to 5 years, after which you will have a large capital purchase to replace the equipment.

The other major challenge is that you must make a large upfront investment to create the software before you can generate any revenue. This often means that the owner must bring in outside investors who want partial or total control over the business. This adds another layer of complexity compared to selling a service or a physical product.

You can sell information as a product.

In this case, you create a product based on your expertise or skill set, package it, and deliver it as a book, DIY project, or course. In many cases, it can be sold and delivered online.

The beauty of this model is that the biggest cost to develop the content is your time and effort, but once you create the product, it can be sold at scale. This is a big improvement over the service business model where you have competitive pressures that limit the amount you can mark up the labor, and employee recruiting which hinders scalability.

Informational products also avoid many of the challenges of selling physical products, as there is no inventory to finance or manage, no obsolete or damaged products, and returns are generally just a credit card refund process.

Informational products also have the same scalability of software without all the upfront investment or labor costs, management headaches, or investor issues. For all these reasons informational products can be a great choice requiring little investment or financial risk. You can create the product while keeping your day job, and then transition to full-time once you have sales to support your income needs.

You can purchase an existing business.

As the current generation of businessowners begin to retire, we must ensure that these important businesses are passed on to new owners who are equipped to grow and nurture them. There are many businesses to choose from, too.

Many provide great cashflow and are simple businesses to operate.

In most cases, the current owners are willing to finance the purchase. They are usually looking for cashflow for their retirement and do not need a lump sum payout. There are also tax advantages to the seller to make it an installment sale. This is a great opportunity to consider as you look for ways to provide income for your family. Developing a second income stream will also help insulate you from the effects of a large layoff in your industry, or other unforeseen events.

> **"** As the current generation of businessowners begin to retire, we must ensure these important businesses are passed on to new owners who are equipped to grow and nurture them.

The Parallel Economy

The idea of building a parallel economy, where patriots trade with each other, will be key to our future security. It will add a new level of resilience that doesn't exist in our current global corporate structures and supply chains. Buying and selling locally will strengthen our economies and help us avoid another rust belt phenomenon, where manufacturing was purposely offshored to weaken our economy, gut our cities, provide extra profits for the globalist companies, and weaken our national security.

We all became aware of the delicate nature of global supply chains during the recent pandemic. It was a rude awakening when we realized that most of our medicines were sourced from China, and they were not available when needed.

We must learn from these past mistakes. We must ensure that we can manufacture all that we need within our country's borders. There is no need to be dependent for food, energy, or goods from other nations. This is not to say that we shouldn't have international trade, but that we should not be dependent on them for our critical needs.

As a strong independent nation, we will be in a great position to share our innovations, products, and services with others. In our modern world, it is easy for small business to have international trading relationships, as products can easily be shipped around the world and many services can be delivered remotely.

Another important part of our economy is the means of exchange that we use to transact business between individuals or organizations.

The US Federal Reserve Note is currently the global reserve currency of the world and has been since the Bretton Woods Agreement was signed in July 1944 by forty-four countries, toward the end of World War II. At which time the United Kingdom's Pound lost its status as the global reserve currency. Under this new agreement the US dollar (i.e., the Federal Reserve Note) was backed by gold, and all other currencies were pegged to the US dollar. The US dollar could be directly exchanged for gold. The world began trading in dollars and holding their wealth in dollars. This created a deep liquid pool of funds that facilitated world trade.

This worked for a while, but the US took advantage of their reserve currency status and began to print more dollars than they had gold to back them. As a nation, we would purchase goods from other countries and pay them with dollars. They would store their profits in US dollars because of the liquidity that dollars provided, allowing them to easily trade them as needed with other countries. Once these countries realized we were printing more dollars and reducing the value of the reserves they held, they began to trade their dollars for gold as per the Bretton Woods Agreement. This was quickly draining the gold reserves that the US held.

In 1971, Richard Nixon closed this gold window, meaning we broke our commitment in the Bretton Woods agreement and refused to allow other countries to trade their dollars for gold. This was outright criminal.

At that point in time, the Federal Reserve Note became a full fiat currency, meaning it was not backed by anything tangible, just the promise of the US government. Once the United States was off the gold standard, there was no limit to the money printing, as the Federal Reserve Bank was not required to have gold reserves to back the dollars. In order to force other countries to use these new fiat dollars, the United States cut a deal with Saudi Arabia that we would provide military support to them in exchange for them selling their oil in dollars. This was the creation of the Petro Dollar.

All countries that needed oil would be forced to buy dollars to pay for their oil. This was the way that the Federal Reserve extended the life of the Federal Reserve Note as the global reserve currency. This allowed the United States to get cheap products from all over the world, and then dilute the value of the dollars that countries received for their goods.

Said another way, our main export to the world was inflation! However, after playing this game for many decades, the Federal Reserve Note has now lost 99% of its buying power since it was created in 1913.

We are now reaching the end game of the Federal Reserve Note. Many countries are refusing to accept US dollars as payment for their goods. China and Russia have led the way in creating the BRICS nations. They originally consisted of Brazil, Russia, India, China, and South Africa. Many other nations are joining this new association. The only thing that has kept the dollar afloat is the fact that all other fiat currencies around the world are even weaker than the US dollar and the US dollar still has liquidity for now.

Russia recently went back on the gold standard for their ruble, which makes it one of the strongest currencies in the world today.

Because of all this turmoil with the US dollar and other fiat currencies, we will need new currencies and payment systems to support our businesses.

What is money?

Money must have several key attributes:

1. **Medium of Exchange:** Used to facilitate trade, avoiding cumbersome bartering.
2. **Store of Value**: A way to defer use of your wealth to a future date.
3. **Unit of Account**: Used to track and measure value between goods, services, and assets.

4. **Interchangeable:** Every unit is the same as every other unit, unlike real estate where every property is different and not easily compared.

Other attributes include recognizable, durable, portable, divisible, and not easily counterfeited.

Many have had hopes that crypto currencies could be the solution. They will be part of the solution, but it is important that we make a quick distinction between different crypto currencies. There are two main types—Proof of Work and Proof of Stake.

Proof of Work is like mining for gold. You must expend money and energy to get gold out of the ground. As a result, the gold has intrinsic value, as it is worth at minimum the costs expended.

Bitcoin is a Proof of Work coin that requires special computer equipment and energy to "mine" the Bitcoin. Bitcoin then has intrinsic value because of the costs expended. It is a digital store of value.

Proof of Stake allows coins to be created without any costs. These coins can be easily created and, therefore, there is no constraint. And just like fiat currencies, unlimited quantities create inflation and destroy the underlying value.

Another key distinction is that Bitcoin has been determined by the IRS to be a commodity asset, just like gold, because there is no company that controls Bitcoin.

Other crypto currencies are all controlled by companies that determine how many coins will be created and who they will be distributed to. The founders generally create a large number for themselves, diluting the overall value through this inflationary process of creating coins without any invested value. As a result, these alt coins (alternates to Bitcoin) have been deemed to be securities by the Securities Exchange Commission or SEC.

The SEC is currently litigating against many of these companies because they did not follow any SEC guidelines or regulations required for securities as they launched their coins. Most of these companies will not be able to afford the costs or retroactively be able to reach out to all the coin holders and go through the formal SEC regulations to make these transactions legal. This will likely be the end of many of the 24k+ coins that have been created! Meanwhile, the Bitcoin network is getting more secure, more decentralized, and more resilient to attacks.

Bitcoin has a built-in cap of 21,000,000 coins. Once they are fully mined, there will be no additional coins … ever! This makes Bitcoin a great store of value with zero inflation.

Bitcoin is divisible to eight decimal places. One Satoshi is equal to .00000001 Bitcoin. Unlike the dollar that is only divisible to two decimal places, with one cent equal to .01 dollars. This makes Bitcoin extremely divisible.

Bitcoins are interchangeable with any other Bitcoin. It is a unit of measurement. Bitcoin is a medium of exchange. It is recognizable, durable, portable, and not easily counterfeited. It has never been hacked since launched on January 9th, 2009. Bitcoin can be sent anywhere in the world, at any time, in any amount, to anyone at virtually zero cost. You can securely carry any amount of Bitcoin across international borders at any time without risk of confiscation (it doesn't get more portable that that). Bitcoin cannot be manipulated or controlled directly by any government or bank.

> **"** Bitcoin can be sent anywhere in the world, at any time, in any amount, to anyone at virtually zero cost.

The globalist cabal has been able to manipulate the price via centralized exchanges and the futures market, but decentralized exchanges and peer to peer transactions function today and will help us avoid this going forward. Plus, most of the exchanges will collapse due to fraud, as they have sold more coins, including Bitcoin, than they have in their possession. Once people realize that the exchanges are playing the same game that central banks are playing with their currencies, people will pull their coins off the exchanges, and they will collapse.

As the fiat currencies, including the current US dollar (i.e., the Federal Reserve Note), collapse, we will likely see a new US dollar backed by gold and silver or, at minimum, we will return to gold and silver coins for local transactions. We will also see Bitcoin and possibly a few other coins, such as Litecoin, used for local, national, and international transactions.

The lightning network that supports these transactions is becoming more robust every day and can settle high volumes of transactions nearly instantly. This should give us a combination of digital and analog currencies that we can use to run our businesses.

Entrepreneurs and Engineers are the problem solvers of the world. We need more of both.

> **"** Entrepreneurs and Engineers are
> the problem solvers of the world.
> We need more of both.

They look for gaps in current products, services, or solutions and create unique offerings that meet these needs. Sometimes they recombine existing ideas and solutions, and sometimes they create unique new solutions. They often see what we cannot imagine.

For example, Steve Jobs saw the need to create a smartphone with a touch screen when blackberries were all the rage. Getting rid of the keyboard opened space on the device for numerous new possibilities. Buttons could appear when needed for a particular function, and then disappear when no longer needed. What a brilliant idea!

I recall Steve Ballmer, the failed successor to Bill Gates as CEO of Microsoft, bragging on day one of the new iPhone release how Microsoft had sold millions of smartphones and Apple had not even sold one yet. He held up his hand, making a big zero with his fingers to emphasize the point. His lack of vision quickly became obvious, and his arrogant comments showed his lack of respect for his more innovative competitor.

It would be hard now to imagine being restricted to fixed keys with limited functionality. In this case, consumers didn't know what they really needed until Entrepreneurs and Engineers created the future and presented this elegant new solution.

How many future innovations await the talents of Entrepreneurs and Engineers to see a need and fill it?

So, what does it take to become an entrepreneur? And how do you go from problem to solution? These are great questions that deserve detailed answers.

> **❝** Key traits that will help you become a successful Entrepreneur – Be observant, develop problem-solving skills, develop sales skills, be resilient, be resourceful, get along with others, and follow your passion.

First, there are several key traits that will help you become a successful Entrepreneur:

1. **Be observant.** As you experience life, look for problems that cause you or others frustration. Listen to people, talk to people. This is how you will find real-world problems that need solutions.

2. **Develop good problem-solving skills.** Defining the problem in detail brings clarity and deeper understanding of the issue or problem. Identify any underlying assumptions you are making in your analysis. If you can find relevant data, this can also aid your understanding. Before you can ever solve a problem, you must understand the issues clearly.

3. **Develop sales skills.** Entrepreneurs are constantly selling—selling people on your idea, selling investors to fund your idea, and selling customers to buy your

products or services. In the first years, you will spend about 80% of your time selling. This skill is critical. Do not try to delegate this to others. They will never have the same passion you do for your idea!

4. **Be resilient.** Things never go as originally planned. You will have setbacks and disappointments. You will get discouraged and want to quit. This will not feel good. You may start to question if your idea has any merit. You will question your ability to pull it off.

5. **Be resourceful.** Restraints can be your friend. Limited time, money, and other resources cause us to be frugal, creative, and scrappy. Use this to your advantage. Boot strap. As they said in the movie *Red*, "Never underestimate what a small, dedicated team can accomplish."

6. **Learn to get along with others.** People like doing business with people they like. Be genuinely interested and learn to build rapport when meeting new people. While we think we use logic to make our decisions, we use our emotions as a gut check when making decisions. Your future investors and customers are real people, so building relationships with them can add richness to your experience and profits to your bottom line.

7. **Follow your passion.** Your passion is the only thing that will keep you motivated to press forward through the challenges you will face. You must have a strong "why" or you will not make it all the way to the success you

desire. With a strong why, you will not let anything get in the way of reaching your dreams.

Become a good Problem Solver

1. Identify the problem in sufficient detail so you have a clear understanding of the need. Talk to people; read between the lines to get to their true need. We have all heard that people don't want the drill; they want the hole. Probe for additional understanding.

2. Once you have a clear understanding of the problem, you can begin to consider solutions. If the problem is complex, then break it into smaller components to help you simplify this process.

3. At this point, you need to engage your creativity. No idea should be excluded at this stage of your brainstorming. You want to consider every possibility that comes to mind.

4. Once you have multiple potential solutions, you can begin to evaluate each one by defining criteria for how well the solution will solve the problem, including considering the costs of various solutions.

5. Once you lock in on the solution that best solves the problem at a reasonable cost, you move to the next phase. Here, you begin to expand of the various ways that you could implement the proposed solution. With a physical product, this might be the different materials or

manufacturing processes that could be used, or the different ways to sell and distribute the product.

Note: Think of this as an hourglass. The top half is where you brainstorm all the possible solutions. The narrow middle is your defining criteria that limits the ideas that get through. The bottom of the hourglass is where you now consider all the ways to implement the proposed solution. This iterative expand-contract approach allows you to move quickly through the process, always moving forward through each step from ideation to selling your product.

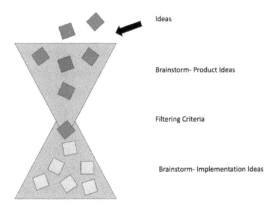

6. Once you are clear on how you would implement your proposed solution, you can begin to prototype the solution. This is where mockups or a working model are developed.

7. Testing comes next. While you can include potential buyers at the earlier stages in your ideation process, you certainly will want to get some feedback from them at this stage of the process. See how they interact with your product and if it appears intuitive to use or operate. You only get one chance to observe them in their initial ignorance. Once they learn the workarounds, they rarely question why it works the way it does. Their initial feedback is gold. Iterate on the feedback you receive and test again with new subjects.

8. Nail it then scale it. Once you are consistently getting positive feedback on all the key functionality, you are ready to produce it for your market. You will never feel totally ready for this phase. The army has a methodology they call "80% and go." They do extensive planning to get 80% of the solution, and then finish the final 20% as they move forward, getting real-world experience and iterating on the fly.

9. Now comes the scary part—marketing. Time to introduce your new baby to the world! You pray they don't tell you your baby is ugly. Be open-minded to the feedback you receive. Be objective. Most products go through several iterations to make improvements after the initial launch. These important tweaks can give years of extended life to your product.

Using this process will allow you to develop a capacity for innovation and creativity than can provide products, services, and revenue that will sustain your business over time. Having a repeatable process will give you confidence that you can adapt to changing demands and market conditions.

Small business is the growth engine of a thriving economy. They provide many important products and services, drive innovation, allow us to create an independent and strong middle class, and develop cashflow and wealth that can be used to bless the lives of our families, as well as others.

Therefore, We Shall Rebuild Our Economies.

> **"** Small businesses allow us to create an independent and strong middle class.

WE SHALL REBUILD OUR ECONOMIES –
SMALL BUSINESS CHALLENGE

Research and identify three ideas for businesses that you and/or your family could launch either online or in your community. List the following for each opportunity:

1. Unmet need your product of service would fill.
2. Research key words online to see if others are delivering a similar product or service and detail what you find.
3. Analyze their offers and pricing. Would you be drawn to their product? Describe what you like and what you would do differently.
4. Develop a bootstrapping plan that would require little capital.
5. Can you presell the product to test the market before you create your product?
6. Can you create your product "on demand" to avoid inventory costs?
7. Can you deliver the service to a prospective customer for free and get their feedback?
8. Talk to 3 to 5 people about your idea to test their reaction and get further feedback.
9. Continue to develop each idea unless you come to an insurmountable showstopping roadblock.
10. Plan at least one next step for further research.

Note: Always spend your time before you spend your money on an idea.

WE SHALL FEAR NO OPPRESSOR

Freedom of thought is at the core of Personal Freedom. All actions are the children of our thoughts. They lead to our decisions, practices, habits, and destiny. It is the right and obligation of every man and woman to take personal responsibility for their choices, including living with the consequences of those choices. This is core to the personal sovereignty and freedom of every living soul. No Man, or Institution created by man, has any right to take away or infringe on our Personal Freedom.

> **"** No Man, or Institution created by man, has any right to take away or infringe on our Personal Freedom.

However, living in a society does require a few simple guidelines to ensure security and fairness for all. These three guidelines have been proven across many cultures and millennia. They have become known as common law.

They are:

1. You must not hurt or kill another human.
2. You must not damage or destroy another's property.
3. You must not steal another's property.

Simple? Yes. Hard to understand? No. And yet the consistent application of these three simple guidelines often eludes us. Our corrupt leaders start wars, leading to the deaths of countless millions. They steal property from one group and give it to another, most often themselves. They impose burdensome taxes that are simply another form of theft. They overregulate so many aspects of our lives that we are suffocated and exhausted. They limit our choices in healthcare, education, and dang near everything else. They often refer to themselves as the Elite (self-appointed). They thrive on the pain and suffering of the people while they live in luxury from the spoils of their wars and theft. The arrogance and hypocrisy of their actions knows no bounds.

All this corruption must be cleaned out like pus from an infected wound, if we are to heal as a society. We have all heard that evil prevails when good men do nothing. We must acknowledge that, after many decades of the Elites' control, this is where we find ourselves.

We must understand how the money system really works. How the control that the banking cabal has had over us since 1871 when after the civil war, the European bankers agreed to loan the US money in return for us setting up the District of Columbia as a separate country within our country. We must understand that the Federal Reserve is not a government entity, but a private bank owned by several large banks that are controlled by a small group of globalist cabal families. We must understand that it was created in secret meetings held on Jekyll Island off the coast of Georgia in 1909.

We must understand that the Sixteenth Amendment authorizing Income Tax was fraudulently implemented and was never ratified! We must understand that they orchestrated these two control mechanisms at the same time to put us in debt as a country by charging us interest on our own money. Money that our Constitution clearly states is to be issued and controlled by our government. Then they take our hard-earned income through income taxes to pay interest on the debt to the bankers. We must understand that our founding fathers wanted to keep the Federal government small and the States strong. The entire federal government was to be funded with import tariffs from other countries, not by taxing citizens.

We must understand that Covid 19 was a planned event by the Globalists, and that they did a test run in September 2019 before releasing the pandemic on the world. We must realize that John Hopkins University built the tracking tools to show the impact of the planned release long before the release, and they were part of the pre-exercise. We must understand that they misused a test—the PCR test—to inflate the numbers of cases, making it appear that it was a serious pandemic. The creator of the PCR test publicly stated that this tool was being misused by the medical industry! We must understand that they purposely brought sick patients into nursing homes to increase the death count of the old and weak among us. We must understand that they shut down the use of Ivermectin and Hydroxychloroquine (HCQ) because these inexpensive medicines would have easily treated the problem since they had both been used for decades to kill similar parasites.

We must understand that the entire exercise was designed to give them authority to shut down our economies, allowing only the globalist companies to remain open for business. This was part of their plan to crush the middle class and create a larger dependent class that is easily controlled. Next, they diluted our money when they printed trillions to give to the newly created dependent class.

To take back our Personal Freedom, we must recognize that their authority is a fraud imposed on all of us. They have no right to control, tax, or oppress us in any way. This is a keen insight that must be understood. They have no right to send our children to wars that they created for their personal gain. They have no right to declare themselves our masters.

Our founding fathers understood this well. They lived through tyranny and knew it intimately. In our Declaration of Independence, they stated that when the government oppresses the people, the people have a duty and obligation to throw off the old government and establish a new one.

We don't need a new Constitution; we simply need to enforce the one we have. All laws that are contrary to our constitution are by definition null and void as the higher law will always apply. We need not obey them as they are not valid and have no authority over us.

In recent years, our government has also enforced medical tyranny over us. Vaccine mandates and travel restrictions are a clear violation of our fundamental rights. Saying they are doing it "for our safety" is not valid justification, as we are each individually responsible for making those decisions and our governments should not be interfering with our personal decisions. Freedom of choice for women wanting an abortion but not for other medical procedures, like choosing whether you want to get a vaccination, is nonsensical and ludicrous.

> **❝** We don't need a new
> Constitution; we simply
> need to enforce the one
> we have.

Then there is the shaming and intimidation pushed by woke corporations, unelected NGOs, and the media who are completely owned and controlled by the globalists. Add to this the social media conglomerates who are working with our government to censor free speech and decide what we can talk about. They shadow ban and outright cancel any dissenting voices.

This is not the America our forefathers fought for. This is the exact opposite of the free speech that our first amendment ensures. How did we let these tyrants gain this kind of control over us?

They have pushed political correctness and virtue signaling to the point that many are afraid to stand up for what is right and defend our freedoms. When did we become such cowards? We are the only nation on Earth who has these freedoms codified into our Constitution. If we can't defend our freedoms, then the rest of the world is doomed as they don't have these fundamental protections in place.

People around the world are looking to us as the beacon of hope in a world of tyranny and oppression. Once gone, it will be hard to regain this lost ground. We really need to become aware of our situation and the precarious position we find ourselves in.

If the globalists can get their carbon tax, they will be able to tax us for everything we do, including breathing! This is the ultimate tax, as they can use it to justify anything they want to accomplish.

Add to this the Central Bank Digital Currencies (CBDCs) that they are working to implement. This is programmable money completely controlled by the government. They can tie it to social credit scores, and if we do not do what they command, they would be able to cut us off from purchasing food, traveling, or any other thing they deem as inappropriate. This would be used in conjunction with the carbon tax to control every aspect of our lives.

This is their goal. This is their plan. They have it well documented on the World Economic Forum's website. They absolutely believe that they should decide who lives and who dies. Their stated goal is to reduce the population by 90%. This is a level that they believe the earth can sustain. They want a small slave class and the elite class. They don't want the rest of us using what they believe to be their resources.

This is Satan's plan for God's children. To turn the entire Earth into a prison where all personal freedoms have been removed. If you read the Communist Manifesto, you will see that they need to accomplish three big goals to ensure their total control.

- Abolish Gun and Property Rights.
- Abolish the family and replace its function with the State.
- Abolish God and replace Him with State worship, and eventually direct worship of Satan.

With their agenda in mind, we can clearly see the many ways they are working to accomplish these goals. Notice how the events happening each week can be aligned into these three buckets.

> **"** Evil attempts to control and enslave us, but God is on our side, and God wins.

This is Satan's plan. He promises his servants money, power, and fame in return for supporting his plan. We must not allow this to happen! America has always been intended by God to be free so long as we honor and worship Him. We know how this battle ends. We understand that God is in control and, in the end, will banish Satan and his minions to a place we call hell, where they will not be able to rage war against us for all eternity.

We must stay on the right side of this battle. We are accountable to our God who created us and unconditionally granted us our agency and personal freedom. When we reach the end of our lives, it is only God's judgment that we need be concerned about.

Evil attempts to control and enslave us, but God is on our side, and God wins.

Therefore, We Shall Fear No Oppressor.

WE SHALL FEAR NO OPPRESSOR CHALLENGE

1. Read the Declaration of Independence (back of the book).
2. List five of the patriot's grievances that stand out to you.
3. Read the first ten amendments to the Constitution, known collectively as "The Bill of Rights" (back of the book).
4. Map the Founding Fathers list of their grievances with the specific amendment in the Bill of Rights that would have protected them.
5. List your top five grievances with our current government.
6. Map your grievances with the specific amendment in the Bill of Rights that should protect you.

WE SHALL LEAD WITH INTEGRITY

Integrity is when our thoughts, words, and actions are in harmony with each other. Moral Integrity is when all three are aligned with righteous principles and actions.

A hermit living in total isolation may not need to develop moral integrity as he, and he alone, would benefit or suffer from his choices. When we introduce a second person, then the hermit's actions can impact them, and the hermit now has a moral responsibility not to infringe on their rights or ability to choose.

When we scale this simple example to a community, nation, or the whole world, the complexities grow dramatically.

> **"** Integrity is when our thoughts, words, and actions are in harmony with each other. Moral Integrity is when all three are aligned with righteous principles and actions.

Consider the typical politician. It is easy for them to tell the people what they want to hear in order to get the votes, but when it is time to deliver on their promises, they usually fall short and disappoint. It is easy to make a promise. You often feel a small sense of satisfaction just from making the promise because the person or group receiving the promise is happy and you feel good just for making it. There is no problem with making promises, the problem is in keeping them!

Whenever you over commit and underdeliver, you will disappoint and even anger those promised. It is therefore important that you only make promises that you can keep! If the promise has a deadline attached to it, make sure that you allow a cushion, because other priorities will inevitably compete with your promise. It doesn't matter if it is a small promise made to a child, or a big promise made to a large group, if you fail to deliver, the result is the same. People quickly learn that you cannot be counted on to deliver what you said you would, when you said you would, and your personal integrity is damaged.

Leaders with low moral integrity often justify breaking their promises because they rationalize other priorities outrank the commitments they made previously. They may also callously believe that their position of power allows them to break promises without fear of reprisal. One thing all leaders must realize is: to be a leader, you must have willing followers!

> ❝ One thing all leaders must realize is to be a leader you must have willing followers.

People are motivated by three key things: Fear, Duty and Love. Fear is the weakest motivation, as it requires constant coercion and reinforcing to maintain its power. Duty is a stronger form of motivation; people will do things they would normally not even consider (i.e., soldiers will go to war to fulfill their duty to their country, even though they have no desire to leave their families, travel halfway around the world, and fight or kill other people they had no personal disagreement with!). Love is, of course, the strongest motivation known to Man. A mother or father would gladly lay down their lives to protect their beloved children.

Moral Integrity is also a key basis for trade. For example, if a company is lacking moral integrity in the production and delivery of their products or services, then they will not be trusted by their customers or trading partners. Without trust, they will struggle to be competitive, as they will either lose the sale or be required to prove that the quality is as stated. Additional validation and verification add friction in terms of both money and time. For these reasons Moral Integrity in business is good for business!

> **" The strongest leaders honor and love those they lead and serve.**

The strongest leaders honor and love those they lead and serve. Their genuine caring is sensed and recognized by their followers who are willing to be led because they trust the leader. Weak leaders must constantly apply force through fear, coercion, or false promises to get their desired behaviors. This is never sustainable because it is weak when up against the innate human drive for freedom.

Align your leadership with correct principles, honor your team's right to personal choice, create a vision based on Freedom and Prosperity, and you will have willing followers.

The servant leader model is proven to draw in willing followers who will support your cause. When you show them, by example, that you practice the same behaviors that you hope they will emulate, you give them a pattern to follow.

It has been said that employees will treat your customers the same way that you treat your employees. If you show caring, respect, and a willingness to ensure their needs are met, they will do the same with their fellow team members and your customers. If you show a genuine interest in their lives and the issues they are facing and build personal relationships, then you will have higher client retention as your customers are treated the same way.

I once worked as a Regional VP for a large public company based out of Houston. I was personally responsibility for $335 million in revenue with 2,500 employees across seventeen states. We had three other Regional VPs who were my peers.

I was at a celebration where the Regional VP of the year was getting an award in front of the entire senior leadership team. I was not the recipient and was in the back of the room with some of the C-suite team members. As my friend was getting his award and feeling great about his success, having his hard work and efforts being recognized, they told me, while chuckling, that they planned on laying him off the next day! I was shocked that they would do this to him. They were so disingenuous to have this celebration, knowing what they planned to do. They showed me their true colors and their lack of moral integrity. I gave my notice the next week!

Contrast this example with another I personally experienced. The pandemic hit the travel industry on Friday March 13th, 2020 when international travel was shut down by our government. I worked at my brother's travel management company as a C-suite executive. We were booking $700 million in travel. Within forty-eight hours, our revenues dropped below zero, as we had to pay out millions in refunds without any revenue. We only had contingency plans for a 10 to 30% drop in business (that lesson had been learned from the 2008 Great Recession). However, never in our wildest dreams could we imagine a 100%+ drop in revenue. What should we do?

Over that weekend, a plan was devised. The goals were threefold:

1. Protect our clients.
2. Protect our company.
3. Save as many jobs as possible.

The following Monday, March 17th, was a tough day. We had always had a high employee retention rate with a list of applicants who wanted to join the company at any time. For the first time in thirty years of steady growth, we had to lay off good people. 50% of our workforce of 500 were laid off or furloughed that day.

My brother cried! He never cries.

The next day a 5.7 magnitude earthquake hit Salt Lake City, shaking our corporate headquarters and causing us to quickly exit the building. Holy crap! It felt like the world was ending! Not normally superstitious, we couldn't help but wonder what the third disaster would be. Fortunately, it didn't come as an abrupt disaster.

We hunkered down and planned to ride it out. My brother took a 100% pay cut. The executive team took a 50% pay cut. The remaining employees took a 25% pay cut. But we were still employed. We were extremely busy processing refunds and helping our clients unwind their travel programs, but we were not getting paid for any of this work. At the time, we were all being told by the government "just two weeks to flatten the curve." What really happened was an agonizingly slow and painful recovery period that was spread over two and a half years.

My brother never wavered in his commitment to our employees or our clients. He invested additional funds to ensure that we had the cashflow to continue operations. And, as soon as he was able, he reinstated full salaries. In addition, he implemented a "shared sacrifice" bonus program that would make up the lost wages with higher future bonuses. We rehired many of those who had been furloughed, and he increased the level of communication to our employees, keeping them informed as to our progress and financial stability to help alleviate fears. Our team was strengthened as we worked together to get through this existential challenge to the business.

Now that is leadership! Doing the right thing when it is hard to do.

> " The people of the world are tired of morally bankrupt leaders who focus on their own personal gain

We Shall Lead with Integrity

The people of the world are tired of morally bankrupt leaders who focus on their own personal gain at the expense of those they lead. They are tired of large corporations laying off tens of thousands of hard-working employees, and then turning around and paying themselves large bonuses! A hunger for money and power drives their decisions.

Their time must come to an end. There is a worldwide need for new leaders with moral integrity. We need to step up and be those leaders!

Therefore, We Shall Lead With Integrity.

WE SHALL LEAD WITH INTEGRITY
CHALLENGE

1. Identify and list ten potential circumstances where you might have an opportunity to Lead with Integrity.
2. Write out your predetermined response to each situation.
3. Describe three times when you passed an integrity test at some time in your life.
4. List an example of a time you failed to show integrity when a situation arose and describe how you felt inside.
5. Write a commitment statement detailing how you will respond when future situations arise.

WE SHALL HONOR GOD

All that we have and all that we are is a direct gift from GOD. He is our Father and our Creator. While we may sometimes feel like small specks of life in the immense spinning universe, He has endowed us with a conscience and agency, the gift of Choice. He has given us the gift of life, the ability to love, and to create our own posterity so that we can feel the joy of creation. He has given us families for strength and support. He has given us work so that we can feel the joy of accomplishment.

He has given the two great commandments which are:

1. Love God.
2. Love Your Neighbor.

> **"** He has given us the gift of life, the ability to love, and to create our own posterity so that we can feel the joy of creation.

We show our love to God by loving and serving His children—our neighbors. Therefore, we refer to charity as the pure love of God, because we are helping those who cannot help themselves.

There are many opportunities to do this in each of our everyday lives. Providing food and shelter to the homeless, helping a person with a flat tire, holding the door for another, grocery shopping for the elderly, and shoveling snow for a neighbor are just a few of the simple yet loving ways that we can help another in need. If you consciously look for opportunities, you will find them everywhere.

I am a member of the Church of Jesus Christ of Latter-Day Saints, traditionally referred to as the "Mormons." In our church, members voluntarily donate 10% of their gross earnings to the church—tithings. The funds are used to build chapels and temples and support many good causes and charities.

We also have a welfare program called "Fast Offerings" where members fast (go without food or drink) once a month for twenty-four hours. We then donate the cost of the meals saved, plus more if you wish, to help feed those in need. The funds are first used in our local community, then roll up to be used at the regional level, and then, if there is still excess available, they roll up to the general funds of the church and are distributed worldwide. This is an amazing program that blesses the lives of many people around the world every day.

I am grateful to know that my small sacrifices contribute to the greater cause of feeding God's children wherever they may be.

Many other religious organizations have charitable programs, as well, including homeless shelters and food kitchens. I just happen to be more familiar with those of my church.

The key point is: charity is best provided by individuals, families, churches, and other charities. Governments should not be in the business of charity. They have a track record of mishandling, misusing, and even stealing funds intended to go to those in need. God will not look down on them with kindness.

Honoring God also means giving Him the credit for our successes. If we begin to believe that we are amazing, and we alone are responsible for our own accomplishments, we begin to become arrogant, lose our humility, and become prideful.

The Bible tells us that pride comes before the fall. When we rely less on His guidance in our lives, we will find that we don't have the same insights and bursts of genius. Matthew 7:7 teaches us: "*Ask, and it shall be given you; seek and ye shall find; knock and it shall be opened unto you.*" This is how we get personal revelation in our lives. This is how we access our Father in heaven and His infinite knowledge and wisdom. We must simply ask.

If you have, or have had, young children, you are aware of how this works. "Dad, is the wind invisible? Dad, is the sun a big ball of fire? Dad, will the sun get wet when it sets on the ocean? Dad, Dad, Dad!"

While we may sometimes tire of their constant questions, their curiosity and desire to understand is an example for all of us to follow as we seek answers in our own lives. We must ask with deliberate intent, expecting to receive the needed guidance. But we must also be patient.

He knows what we need, and when we need it. This life is meant to test and try us; otherwise, we will never learn and grow. We can't ask God to remove our trials and tests, or we will never develop the character traits we are capable of. But He will also never give us trials beyond our capacity to bear. None of us really wants to be required to develop the patience of Job! But, knowing we can bear anything we may face is comforting and can help us when we find ourselves amid one of life's challenging chapters.

> **"** We can't ask God to remove our trials and tests, or we will never develop the character traits we are capable of.

Some people want to believe in God but argue that if there was a God, He would not allow bad things to happen to good people. Why is there so much oppression? Why have generations lived in slavery? Why are the weak and innocent abused? Why do we have so many wars? Why are so many needlessly killed? Why do some die so young? Why, why, why?

We find some answers in the Beatitudes, which are the first part of The Sermon on the Mount. Because Jesus said:

> "Blessed are the poor in spirit,
> for theirs is the kingdom of heaven.
> Blessed are those who mourn,
> for they will be comforted.
> Blessed are the meek,
> for they will inherit the earth.
> Blessed are those who hunger and thirst for righteousness,
> for they will be filled.
> Blessed are the merciful,
> for they will be shown mercy.

> Blessed are the pure in heart,
> for they will see God.
> Blessed are the peacemakers,
> for they will be called children of God.
> Blessed are those who are persecuted because of righteousness,
> for theirs is the kingdom of heaven.
> Blessed are you when people insult you, persecute you and falsely say all kinds of evil against you because of me. Rejoice and be glad, because great is your reward in heaven, for in the same way they persecuted the prophets who were before you."

However, these are good questions and, on the surface, using these arguments to deny God may seem reasonable and logical. We all wish these things were not so, and that conditions on Earth were more peaceful. However, these things exist for two primary reasons.

First, we must have opposition between good and evil. Otherwise, our freedom of choice would be meaningless. If we could only choose good or evil, that would not be real choice. Additionally, our freedom to choose is so important to our eternal progression that God will never take it away from any of us, no matter how much we abuse the privilege.

Secondly, we must learn that we cannot avoid the consequences of our choices and actions. It may seem that some get away with their crimes and atrocities in this life, but none will escape God's view or His judgment.

> ❝Our freedom to choose is so important to our eternal progression that God will never take it away from any of us, no matter how much we abuse the privilege.

Some don't believe in God at all, but rather think that we are a random accident in the universe, that we somehow rose-up from the primordial soup. That life is a series of random accidents, that we have no real purpose or value, and that when this life is over, that is the end of us. I couldn't disagree more with this theory.

I see intelligent design all around me! The richness of our own consciousness and thoughts, our senses that allow us to experience sight, smell, sound, taste, and texture all denote there is a God. The love we feel for our families, the genuine concern we have for others, our innate desire to serve them. Our instinct to build, create, and organize the world around us. All these things tell us that we are children of an intelligent Creator who loves each of us and wants us to learn and grow and become like Him.

Rather than being a random bit of moist dust with a finite lifespan, we are eternal beings having a mortal experience. Our spirits will continue beyond this life. And if you believe in the resurrection, as I do, we will once again have our spirit combined with our body into a glorified immortal being, never to taste death again. This is a vision that should bring hope to all who believe.

Even if my beliefs turned out to be wrong, I would rather live a life of hope and promise. I would rather live as a good person of high moral character, honoring and living correct principles while treating others with kindness and respect. Loving and serving those around me. Working to build my character, be an influence for good to those around me. I would rather live a life of abundance and gratitude.

I want to live my best life possible with the gifts I have been given. I want to be an inspiration to my children. I want my grandchildren to sit on my lap as I teach and inspire them to keep their curiosity alive, follow their passions, and be kind to others. I want my family to remember me as kind and caring, willing to take time for them whenever they needed me. I want them to cherish our memories together and share their favorite stories with their children. I want them to know I love learning. I want them to know I appreciate the sacrifices that my ancestors made to provide the life that I am blessed with today. I want them to know that family relationships are critical to their happiness in this life. I want them to know that building a relationship with their Creator will give them strength to get through challenges and periods of loneliness. I want them to know that they brought joy and meaning to my life. I want them to know all these things and so many more.

So, you see, it doesn't really matter if my beliefs turn out to be wrong. I would still choose to live the life described over a selfish, lonely existence surrounded by my money and the fake friends that it attracts! In the end, we will learn all the mysteries of God and learn the answers to all our deepest questions. That will be amazing!

In the meantime, we get to enjoy all the marvelous creations that are part of our experience here on Earth.

When we leave this mortal life, we will not take our possessions or our money. We will not take power or fame with us. What we will take is our knowledge and wisdom, the character traits that we have developed, and the connections and relationships we have built. These are the real treasures of the Earth! We must all take care that we don't get our priorities mixed up and focus on the wrong things. This is the lesson we must all learn.

God is our Creator. God is our Father. God is good. Everything we have, and everything we are, is a gift from God.

Therefore, We Shall Honor God.

WE SHALL HONOR GOD CHALLENGE

1. Take the Spirituality Assessment (back of the book)
2. Reflect on your personal level of spirituality.
3. Detail in a few paragraphs your beliefs about life, including answering the age-old questions that humanity has asked for millennia: where did we come from? Why are we here? Where are we going after we die?
4. Create a statement to describe your beliefs about God. Share this with your family and discuss each of your beliefs.
5. Reflect on your current spiritual practice and identify three things you would like to improve. For example, you might choose increased prayer, scripture study, church service, or spending more time in nature.
6. Commit thirty minutes each week for a month to implement a spiritual practice in your life.

WE SHALL LEAVE A LEGACY OF FREEDOM

It is amazing that our Founding Fathers accomplished so much in their lives when the average lifespan was only about forty-five years. They learned and achieved so many important things. They were well read and developed many talents. They were farmers, merchants, scientists, inventors, and statesmen. They were engaged in the issues and events of their day. Many of them were young, only in their twenties and thirties, when they were moved by the call to join the cause of Freedom.

Our Founding Fathers suffered much oppression and inequity at the hands of the British monarch, King George III. As outlined in the Declaration of Independence, the British Monarchy and Parliament repeatedly infringed on their rights and freedoms.

A few of their grievances are listed below:

1. Dissolved their Houses of Representatives.
2. Refused to assent to needed laws.
3. Forbid his governors to address pressing issues.
4. Restricted Immigration to America.
5. Kept Standing armies among the people in peacetime.
6. Held mock trials for murders committed by the British.
7. Cut off trade from other parts of the world.
8. Imposed taxes without consent.

9. Denied trial by jury.
10. Waged war against the colonies.
11. Plundered the seas.
12. Ravaged the coastlines.
13. Burned their towns.
14. Hired mercenaries to fight the colonists.
15. Forced captives to bear arms against their countrymen.
16. Forced captives to execute fellow countrymen.

All these grievances were born with patient requests for redress but were answered with repeated injury.

Thomas Paine was one of those patriots who was led to be at the right time and place to make a big impact. His short book, *Common Sense*, was released on January 10th, 1776. This was the same time when King George declared in Parliament that the American Colonists were in direct rebellion.

It was a dangerous time to write and print the book. Most publishers wouldn't touch the project. He found a brave printer named Robert Bell, and they published it anonymously stating that it was "by an Englishman."

At the time, most Americans were still hopeful that they would get concessions for their many grievances from British Parliament. Most were not thinking about forming a new nation and breaking from their common heritage and the most powerful government on Earth.

However, the book was an instant success, selling out the first two printings of thousands of copies, each in a matter of days. Newspapers carried much of the content and nineteen editions made it to print in America and seven British additions, as well as a quick translation into French. It is estimated that it sold 120k copies in just three months and over 500k within the year. This was an amazing feat at the time.

The book made a strong argument for an independent nation and influenced many to join the cause of Freedom. A favorite quote from his book is *"The sun never shone on a cause of greater worth."* The rest, as they say, "is history."

> **"** "The sun never shone on a
> cause of greater worth"
> ~ Thomas Paine

They birthed this nation with their blood, sweat, and tears. They didn't stop because it was too hard. They didn't stop when they lost their businesses and their farms. They didn't stop when their friends and family were wounded or killed. They kept going through the toughest of trials because they believed in the cause of Freedom. They knew they were creating something special that would benefit many generations to come. They knew they were on the right side with God. They knew this was their one chance to create a free nation governed by the People for the People. They left an amazing legacy in our charge.

If we hope to save and extend this legacy, we can no longer be complacent about our Freedoms! It is no longer acceptable to be the silent majority. There is much to be done.

More than ever, you are needed to step up and take more responsibility for our future. Our families need good fathers and mothers. Our communities have been weakened and corrupted, and they need honest, hard-working individuals to lead with integrity.

Our governments at many levels have been infiltrated from within. They are aggressively pushing an agenda that goes against all that we hold dear. From our school boards and county governments to the President of the United States, we have seen this corruption with our own eyes. We all know the difference between good and evil, and we see the progress that evil has made while we were busy living our lives.

Our grandchildren are counting on us to hand the baton of Freedom to them, fully intact, so they can enjoy life, liberty, and the pursuit of happiness, as promised in our founding documents.

We do not want to be the weak link in the chain. We do not want to be the generation that allowed evil to consume our society. We do not want to be the generation that failed to act. Our Freedom is at risk. Our grandchildren's future is at risk. We can be the heroes of the next generation. We can ensure America remains a free country.

Less than 10% of Americans participated in the American Revolution and yet, with their efforts, they created our great nation. Fortunately, our battle need not be fought with guns and swords. Ours is primarily an information war to control the narrative.

We must outwit them, refuse to consent to their control, and overwhelm their evil efforts. We have the high ground. We have the moral authority. We have 80 to 90% of the population on our side. We have God on our side. What are we waiting for?

> " Our grandchildren are counting on us to hand the baton of freedom to them, fully intact, so they can enjoy life, liberty, and the pursuit of happiness.

Freedom of choice and Freedom from oppression are the foundation of a strong and vibrant society. We are the generation who currently has the charge to carry the torch of Freedom forward for future generations.

Therefore, We Shall Leave a Legacy of Freedom.

WE SHALL LEAVE A LEGACY OF FREEDOM CHALLENGE

1. Create a family tree, including your parents, grandparents, and current descendants (worksheet in the back of the book).
2. Write three paragraphs on the lessons you have learned from your grandparents and parents.
3. Write three paragraphs detailing the legacy you will leave to your posterity. Write this in the first-person past tense.

Include:
    1. What you believe.
    2. How you defended our freedoms.
    3. What you expect of them in the future.

ARE YOU READY TO LEAD?

The longer we live, the more we realize just how short this life really is. We have roughly 30,000 days on this Earth. Considering that the first 25% are spent just reaching adulthood, that theoretical age when we should be far enough along on the path from selfish to selfless that we can make a meaningful contribution to society. The last 25% are often spent in slowly declining health and vitality. This leaves us with about 15,000 days, roughly 40 years, to finish our formal educations, get married, raise our families, make an impact in our communities and the world, and Leave Our Legacy. Wasting our time and talents is not a good option.

The forces of evil in the world are ramping up. They are well organized and committed to their vision and plan for total control over us. We see them attacking our money and wealth, our food and energy, our mental and physical health, and our children. It is time for serious reflection on the reality we find ourselves in.

We took for granted that the rights and liberties we have known in our lifetimes would automatically be extended to the next generations. But this is an error in thinking. We are always but one generation away from tyranny, and it always starts with complacency.

I love the quote that "Good times make weak men, weak men create bad times, bad times create strong men, strong men create good times."

> **❝** "Good times make weak men, weak men create bad times, bad times create strong men, strong men create good times."

We are at the point in this cycle where we have had good times, and it has created weak men. Weak in character. Weak in resolve. Weak in action. Weak in understanding.

This weakness has allowed the evil people of the world to flourish and bring upon us the tough times we now find ourselves in. It is time that we become strong again.

This is the time of action. We are NOT talking about aggressive or violent behaviors. We ARE talking about stepping up as good people who care about the future we are leaving to future generations. We ARE talking about making a difference wherever we can. We ARE talking about actively focusing on expanding our circle of influence for good. We ARE talking about finding ways to strengthen our families and be better examples to them. We ARE talking about finding ways to strengthen our communities by serving and getting involved at a local level. As we do this, we will create a groundswell that will be a powerful force against the evil that is rising.

There is much to be done. If you have not taken the challenges at the end of each chapter, please go back and start on them now. These challenges are designed to prepare you to be more engaged in your daily life. To give you the tools and mindset to live your values more fully. To help you be bolder as you interact with others and stand up for your values and the correct principles that help us operationalize them.

> **"** The cause of Freedom is just, and the world needs your unique contribution.

Please ponder what the right path is for you as you think about the Legacy you will leave. We each have been given unique talents and abilities by our Creator. How we choose to use these talents is up to each of us. The cause of Freedom is just, and the world needs your unique contribution. It is time for all of us to Awake and Arise to our potential. It is time for us to lead.

May God bless our efforts!

A Brighter Vision

Many Patriots had lived their entire lives "in the system," trying to be good citizens, employees or businessowners, mothers and fathers. They had saved and invested in all the programs that they were told and believed would provide them with a comfortable retirement. They sent their kids to school, believing they would learn the same correct principles that they were taught in school. They understood that there are only two genders. They trusted that their government and the food and medical industries had their best interest at heart. They grew up believing that America was the "land of the free and the home of the brave." They honored the American flag and felt something special when they put their hand on their heart and sang the national anthem!

> **"** They honored the American flag and felt something special when they put their hand on their heart and sang the national anthem!

Then, in March 2020, their world changed and, suddenly, everything made less sense. They began to question a lot of things. The pandemic created massive fear, but the numbers didn't make sense. There were no real deaths at the time, but they locked down their cities, closed their businesses and schools, and masked everybody while making illegal the simple solutions that had worked for generations. There was never any evidence that there was real science behind these decisions.

There were riots supposedly sparked by race wars, but they were told these were mostly peaceful. However, the left-wing extremists burned and looted the cities, and the police stood by or were defunded to limit their effectiveness.

They witnessed massive fraud in their elections but were told they were the most secure ever. They began to see the lies being told by the media, even though they were delivered with such elegance and conviction that they seem believable. They were told they were causing Climate Change and should reduce their carbon footprint, yet the elites flew around the world in their jets and purchased mansions on the coasts they were saying would be covered in water within a few years. Their hypocrisy knew no bounds, and they spewed on about the sacrifices the people needed to make. None of this made sense, and yet they bombarded the people with these lies hundreds of times a day.

People were wondering what was true. They wanted to understand what was really happening in the world and what they could to do to help their family and friends navigate this world they found themselves in. They were tired of being the Silent Majority!

By the year 2023, the globalist elite pedophiles had infiltrated all levels of government, education, and business. Propaganda kept the people in the dark. The media was controlled by the elites to ensure only their message was heard. Pandemics and terrorism kept everyone in fear so they would look to and trust the globalists and their solutions. Pedophilia and blackmail allowed them to control their puppets in business and government. Bioweapons pitched as vaccines were created to weaken and kill the people. Their goal was to reduce the population to a small elite class and a slave class to serve the elite.

Food destruction was accomplished through sabotage and weather weapons. The middle class was destined for destruction, as were all small businesses and new energy solutions. They had manipulated the children to believe boys were girls and girls were boys; transgenderism was at its peak. Depression and drug addiction ruled the day.

The elites were working hard to take the remaining rights from the people, using the guise of terrorism and mass shooting to take away guns and using the myth of hate speech to take away free speech. 15-minute cities were being developed to control the people and limit their movement and freedom. Travel was banned due to energy restrictions imposed to save the planet from "Climate Change." They controlled energy and food to control the people.

Patriotic Americans longed for the America they grew up in. They longed to provide their kids and grandkids with the idealistic childhood they had enjoyed. They couldn't believe how the world had changed so quickly. Hope was a distant memory and most thought all was lost. The globalists had infiltrated from within and repressed the whole human race. Creativity, innovation, critical thinking, and freedom had been banned.

The Turning Point was when a small group of patriots began to work to restore the freedom we all longed for. A few patriots began to speak out. They were ridiculed and attacked by the media and the globalists, but they would not be deterred. The human drive for personal freedom was the spark that started the revolution.

Small communities of patriots sprang up. Free speech platforms were developed that gave the people a voice. The truth started to seep out of the cracks in the globalist control mechanisms. The globalists system was being exposed and their lies were breaking down.

Brave whistleblowers came forward to expose their crimes. Evidence that had been suppressed by the media and their control mechanisms broke out into the light of day. Their dark crimes against humanity were exposed. The criminals began to turn on each other as they sought to save themselves. Their world crumbled fast!

Once exposed they no longer felt safe in public! They went from being celebrated to being shunned by the society they tried to control. They were now the ones living in fear!

It was in this environment that the Engaged Patriot Community was created. This community gave people a space among like-minded patriots, where they could learn the truth and fill in the gaps in their understanding. Together, they discussed the current issues and banded together to create solutions.

Engaged Patriots Community members began to expand their influence and serve in their local communities. They were united by a common cause and bound by a desire to lead the way in bringing freedom and hope back to the people.

The Engaged Patriots Manifesto was their call to action. Patriots who were tired of being on the sidelines and wanted to get into the game joined the cause. They shared a message of hope and taught correct principles. They led by example in their families and communities. They created a resurgence of the spirit that had made America great in the past. Working hard and taking personal responsibility for their actions was back in style.

As they worked together to reestablish freedom and rebuild communities, their vision of the possible expanded exponentially. The people once again realized that they were created by God to be free and, with that freedom, to create the world that they wanted to live in. Freedom was returning and the world celebrated!

The year is 2030. I am now seventy years old, and my wife and I are in the best shape of our lives! Natural Medicine has helped us restore our health. Our kids and grandkids are thriving! The globalist elite pedophiles have been defeated and have been executed or jailed for life. Freedom has been reborn in America. Kids are learning our true history, and everyone understands the Constitution and cherishes the freedoms it preserves. Income tax has been abolished, along with the Federal Reserve. The US dollar is backed by gold and other natural resources and inflation is nonexistent. We are no longer slaves in the system but rather sovereign individuals. The division and woke-ism pushed by the globalists have been replaced with a new sense of community. We don't have red and blue, black and white … we simply have free Americans.

> **" We don't have red and blue, black and white … we simply have free Americans.**

Manufacturing is thriving, new small businesses are sprouting up everywhere, and the world is full of hope. Products are not being built with planned obsolescence but rather with pride in craftsmanship and durability. Free energy has made so many projects possible.

Savings and investment are at all-time highs, as families can live on a small portion of their income due to the removal of income taxes, payroll taxes, property tax, and all registration and licensing fees. Federal and State governments have been reduced to the bare minimum required to protect our country and ensure law and order. Both violent crimes and petty crimes are at all-time lows, as tough consequences have discouraged criminals.

Local government consists of residents who volunteer their time and otherwise have productive lives. Career politicians no longer exist. Federal and State representatives serve for one term then return to civilian life.

Innovation is exploding as people spend more of their time creating and building value rather than being entertained 24/7 or being a spectator in the lives of celebrities. Poverty is not a thing anymore, as people have become more productive and those few in need are helped at the local level.

Education is also localized with parents running the school boards and approving the curriculum. Christian values have returned, and the Pledge of Allegiance is heard every morning in our schools. Public events and activities start with prayer in honor of God. People are heathy, happy, and productive. Our children are once again safe from predators. Personal Freedom has been restored, and God smiles down on His children!

Matthew J. Cameron
July 4th, 2023

" Freedom has been
restored, and God smiles
down on His children!

WHY ENGAGED PATRIOTS?

I was sick and tired...

ENGAGED PATRIOTS
APR 1, 2023

ENGAGED PATRI☆TS

What was I sick and tired of?

- Sick and Tired of woke-ism permeating our society.
- Sick and Tired of the liberals pushing Socialism and Communism.
- Sick and Tired of the Trans Movement cheating women out of their accomplishments.
- Sick and Tired of liberals confusing our children.
- Sick and Tired of Drag Queens pushing sexualization on our children.

- Sick and Tired of unfair elections where your vote doesn't count.
- Sick and Tired of Fed and Banking Institutions manipulating the economy.
- Sick and Tired of oppressive taxation and theft through inflation.
- Sick and Tired of fake pandemics and medical tyranny.
- Sick and Tired of the one-sided lying media pushing their propaganda.
- Sick and Tired of the CIA and FBI creating false flag events and wars.
- Sick and Tired of Government facilitating Human Trafficking.
- Sick and Tired of Fake Climate Change emergencies.
- Sick and Tired of all infringements of our GOD-given rights.
- Sick and Tired of globalist organizations taking over national sovereignty with their One World Government.
- Sick and Tired of unelected bureaucrats trying to control us.
- Sick and Tired of the infiltration from within corrupting our culture.
- Sick and Tired of the distance we have moved from our Founder's vision.
- Sick and Tired of all the satanic culture around us.
- Sick and Tired that we can't talk to anyone about what we know.

- Sick and Tired of being labeled conspiracy theorists and extremists.
- Sick and Tired of globalist companies with their ESG-Diversity Equity and Inclusion and Sustainability narrative.
- Sick and Tired of the immoral minority trying to control the moral majority!

Was I the only one feeling this way?

I don't think so. I believe there are millions of Americans, just like me, who are worried. Worried that we will lose our freedom, our health, our wealth. Worried that our children and grandchildren will grow up under a totalitarian government. Worried that, with all the inflation and food and energy shortages, we may not be able to feed our families. Worried that our politicians could start a nuclear war that would kill millions.

Because of these concerns and frustrations, I have at different times felt Helpless, Sad, Afraid, Fearful, and Angry.

So, why didn't I do anything about it?

- I didn't know what I could do.
- I didn't want to be exposed to their vicious cancel culture.
- I didn't know if I could make a difference.
- I was busy with work.
- I was busy with my family.
- I didn't know where to start.
- I hoped others might step up to solve the problems.

Then, one morning I had a thought. And that thought stayed in my mind all day long.

I thought that if there were millions just like me with the same frustrations and concerns, and we all stepped up, we could make a massive impact for good in the world! I thought that what we needed was a community that attracted patriots and leaders and a manifesto that inspired us to be more engaged in strengthening our families and our communities. What resulted is the *Engaged Patriots Manifesto* and the *Engaged Patriots Community*.

ENGAGED PATRI☆TS

★ MANIFESTO ★

WE SHALL PROTECT THE WEAK AND INNOCENT
WE SHALL SHOW COMPASSION TO OTHERS
WE SHALL TEACH CORRECT PRINCIPLES
WE SHALL STRENGTHEN OUR FAMILIES
WE SHALL SERVE IN OUR COMMUNITIES
WE SHALL REBUILD OUR ECONOMIES
WE SHALL FEAR NO OPPRESSOR
WE SHALL LEAD WITH INTEGRITY
WE SHALL HONOR GOD
WE SHALL LEAVE A LEGACY OF FREEDOM

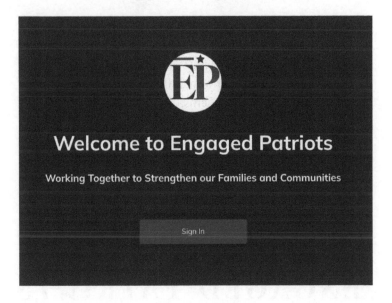

Together, we will…

- Feel more empowered to make a difference.
- Create a better future for our children and grandchildren.
- Spend time in a community with like-minded patriots.
- Better understand the world and how to interpret events.
- Feel empowered to be bolder in our words and actions.
- Be more independent from the globalist control mechanisms.
- Embrace the Manifesto in our daily lives.
- Learn to be critical thinkers and recognize propaganda and lies.
- Engage as leaders in our families and communities.

Why Engaged Patriots?

- Make decisions based on faith, not fear.
- Be part of a community helping each other.
- No longer be part of the silent majority, but be part of the Engaged Patriots Movement.
- Feel more in control of our future.
- Be part of a community that values our contributions.
- Have a strong support structure and learning environment.
- Easily talk to people about the globalist agenda.
- Feel more connected to our Founding Fathers.
- Feel more connected to our Creator.
- Feel more hope.

So, ask yourself the following questions:

- Are you a Patriot?
- Are you tired of the Woke Agenda?
- Are you concerned our Freedoms are at risk?
- Do you want to make a difference?
- Will you leave your family a legacy of Freedom?
- Are you ready to lead?

If your answers to these questions are 100% YES, then you have found your people!

- Who are our people? Patriots.
- Who are not our people? Woke Liberals.

- What is our Cause? Saving Freedom for Future Generations.
- What is our Vision? Convert the Silent Moral Majority into Engaged Patriots.
- What are our Core Values? The ten value declarations in the *Engaged Patriots Manifesto*.
- What is our Mission? Help Patriots embrace and live the ten Declarations in the *Engaged Patriots Manifesto*.
- What is our Strategy? Create a thriving community where Patriots can learn, engage, and Work Together to Strengthen our Families and Communities.

Join us in this important cause. We are committed to the principles of sound money, personal choice, individual responsibility, disciplined work ethic, strong families and communities ... and limited government. We lead by example and focus on expanding our circle of influence for good in the world!

Together, we can regain our freedoms and liberties and leave a better world for our children and grandchildren.

Check out our Engaged Patriots Substack

HELLO PATRIOTS!

What good can we do in the world today?

ENGAGED PATRIOTS
APR 6, 2023

ENGAGED PATRI☆TS

I like to start out with that question because it is our actions and not just our beliefs that will change the world. The Silent but Moral Majority knows that the world is getting more corrupt every day, but they simply don't know how or where they can make a difference, let alone a real impact. Well, the good news is that a lot of small efforts from the Moral Majority will have an enormous impact in our families, communities, and the world at large. We don't all need to do everything, but we all need to do something.

Hello Patriots!

What is at stake? Just our Freedom!

Freedom is a fundamental human right, and its protection is essential for a healthy society. Without freedom, our ability to think, speak, and act freely would be limited and our potential for growth, innovation, and progress would be drastically hindered.

By protecting freedom, we safeguard our rights to develop and express ourselves as individuals, to make choices for our lives, to pursue our passions, and to participate in the political process. We also protect our right to seek equality, justice, and fairness, ensuring that everyone has an equal opportunity to achieve their goals and reach their highest potential. In short, protecting freedom is key to preserving a secure and prosperous society.

Where do we begin?

We begin with ourselves. This is where we will always have the most influence!

Stop and take a few moments to reflect on what you value most. For me, Freedom is at the top of my list of values. How do I define Freedom? I define it as having the flexibility to determine how I spend my time, who I spend my time with, and where I spend my time. So, for me, control over my time and personal choices is the ultimate freedom. Anything that infringes on my ability to choose makes me feel oppressed. I certainly don't need the government or other social institutions telling me what to do, when to do it, or how to do it.

God made us free and gave us the intelligence to make our own choices, and He holds us accountable for the consequences of those choices.

I cringe when bureaucrats try to control me, limit my personal freedom or infringe on my liberties.

I also feel the same way about protecting my loved ones, my property, and my neighborhood. Once we are clear on the values we hold, we can be intentional in applying them in our interactions with others.

The *Engaged Patriots Manifesto* reflects conservative values of personal responsibility and accountability that we can apply in a practical way to guide our daily actions. There are ten declarations in the Manifesto.

ENGAGED PATRIOTS MANIFESTO

1. We Shall Protect the Weak and Innocent.
2. We Shall Show Compassion to Others.
3. We Shall Teach Correct Principles.
4. We Shall Strengthen our Families.
5. We Shall Serve in Our Communities.
6. We Shall Rebuild Our Economies.
7. We Shall Fear No Oppressor.
8. We Shall Lead With Integrity.
9. We Shall Honor God.
10. We Shall Leave a Legacy of FREEDOM.

ENGAGED PATRI☆TS

★ MANIFESTO ★

WE SHALL **PROTECT** THE WEAK AND INNOCENT
WE SHALL **SHOW COMPASSION** TO OTHERS
WE SHALL **TEACH** CORRECT PRINCIPLES
WE SHALL **STRENGTHEN** OUR FAMILIES
WE SHALL **SERVE** IN OUR COMMUNITIES
WE SHALL **REBUILD** OUR ECONOMIES
WE SHALL **FEAR NO OPPRESSOR**
WE SHALL **LEAD** WITH INTEGRITY
WE SHALL **HONOR** GOD
WE SHALL **LEAVE A LEGACY** OF FREEDOM

Do you think it would it make a difference if we all lived these ten values?

Let me know in the comments if you connect to one or more of them.

I believe that if we implement these declarations, we can make a positive impact within our circles of influence and collectively in the world at large. As I said at the start, it is our actions and not just our beliefs that will change the world.

We can start to expand our reach by beginning at home with our families. This is where we can have an immediate impact for good. Simply sharing our values with our families is a great start and a powerful way to let them know what is important to us.

From there, we can show by example that we emulate these values in our daily lives. When our children see that we live our values, they will know how to follow our lead and emulate them in their own lives. For me, this is a top priority if we are to pass on Freedom and the principles of personal responsibility and accountability to the next generation.

In future posts, I will cover these declarations in more detail. Until then, ponder one small thing you can do to make a positive impact today.

Remember, it *always* starts with you!

Check out our Engaged Patriots Substack.

ENGAGED PATRI☆TS

ENGAGED PATRIOTS MANIFESTO -

ASSESSMENT

Instructions: The following assessment is designed to provide feedback on how engaged you are in living the values in the manifesto. Please answer each question truthfully and accurately. Choose the option that best describes you today.

Scoring: Please rate each question on a scale of 1 to 5, with 5 being the highest score.

1 - Never
2 - Rarely
3 - Sometimes
4 - Often
5 - Always

Rate yourself on the 10 declarations:

1. We Shall Protect the Weak and Innocent

1	2	3	4	5

2. We Shall Show Compassion to Others

1	2	3	4	5

3. We Shall Teach Correct Principles

1	2	3	4	5

4. We Shall Strengthen our Families

1	2	3	4	5

5. We Shall Serve in Our Communities

1	2	3	4	5

6. We Shall Rebuild Our Economies

1	2	3	4	5

7. We Shall Fear No Oppressor

1	2	3	4	5

8. We Shall Lead With Integrity

1	2	3	4	5

9. We Shall Honor God

1	2	3	4	5

10. We Shall Leave a Legacy of FREEDOM

1	2	3	4	5

10-17 =In the Stands
18-25=On the Bench
26-33=In the Game
34-41=Scoring Points
42-50=Engaged Patriot

In the Stands - You are a spectator in the game of life!

But seriously, we need you on the team! Our way of life is under attack. The woke liberals are pushing their values on our children. They want our children to believe they are victims and become dependent on the state for support. We need to strengthen our families against this onslaught. They are gutting our communities and putting them at risk with their weak policies on crime and drugs. We need to support and serve in our communities. They are destroying our small businesses and, with it, the middle class. We need to create new businesses that serve fellow patriots. We need you to get involved and support the cause. You can make a difference wherever you are by being a great example to those around you. You understand what is at stake. We cannot let them win without our best efforts to stop the tyranny. Stand up for freedom!

On the Bench - You are on the team but not in the Game.
What is up with that!

But seriously, we need you in the game! Our way of life is under attack. The woke liberals are pushing their values on our children. They want our children to believe they are victims and become dependent on the state for support. We need to strengthen our families against this onslaught. They are gutting our communities and putting them at risk with their weak policies on crime and drugs. We need to support and serve in our communities. They are destroying our small businesses and, with it, the middle class. We need to create new businesses that serve fellow patriots. We need you to get involved and support the cause. You can make a difference wherever you are by being a great example to those around you. You understand what is at stake. We cannot let them win without our best efforts to stop the tyranny. Stand up for freedom!

In the Game - But not scoring any points. Hey, we need some runs!

But seriously, you are in the game but we need more results! Our way of life is under attack. The woke liberals are pushing their values on our children. They want our children to believe they are victims and become dependent on the state for support. We need to strengthen our families against this onslaught. They are gutting our communities and putting them at risk with their weak policies on crime and drugs. We need to support and serve in our communities. They are destroying our small businesses and, with it, the middle class. We need to create new businesses that serve fellow patriots. We need you to get more involved and support the cause. You can make a difference wherever you are by being a great example to those around you. We cannot let them win without our best efforts to stop the tyranny. Stand up for freedom!

Scoring Points-You have delivered some great singles.
Maybe try swinging for the fences!

You are a valued member of the team! Our way of life is under attack. The woke liberals are pushing their values on our children. They want our children to believe they are victims and become dependent on the state for support. We need to strengthen our families against this onslaught. They are gutting our communities and putting them at risk with their weak policies on crime and drugs. We need to support and serve in our communities. They are destroying our small businesses and, with it, the middle class. We need to create new businesses that serve fellow patriots. You are stepping up and supporting the cause. You are making a difference by being a great example to those around you. We cannot let them win without our best efforts to stop the tyranny. Continue to stand up for freedom!

Engaged Patriot - "Woo! We've got a true patriot on our hands. Nice home run! You're actively involved and making a difference. Keep up the amazing work!"

We are grateful that you are on the team! Our way of life is under attack. The woke liberals are pushing their values on our children. They want our children to believe they are victims and become dependent on the state for support. We need to strengthen our families against this onslaught. They are gutting our communities and putting them at risk with their weak policies on crime and drugs. We need to support and serve in our communities. They are destroying our small businesses and, with it, the middle class. We need to create new businesses that serve fellow patriots. We need you to continue to lead and support the cause. You are making a difference by being a great example to those around you. You understand that we cannot let them win without our best efforts to stop the tyranny. Thanks for standing up for freedom!

Join-Engage-Belong

ENGAGED PATRI☆TS

21 Principles Assessment

Instructions: The following assessment is designed to provide feedback on how consistently you live these principles. Please answer each question truthfully and accurately. Choose the option that best describes your current behaviors.

Scoring: Please rate each question on a scale of 1 to 5, with 5 being the highest score.

1 - Never / Not Applicable
2 - Rarely
3 - Sometimes
4 - Often
5 – Always

1. Do you Speak the Truth?

1	2	3	4	5

2. Do you Honor Your Commitments?

1	2	3	4	5

3. Do you Seek Wisdom?

1	2	3	4	5

4. Do you Take Responsibility?

1	2	3	4	5

5. Do you Seek Understanding?

1	2	3	4	5

6. Do you Respect Others?

1	2	3	4	5

7. Are you Humble?

1	2	3	4	5

8. Do you Practice Patience?

1	2	3	4	5

9. Do you Show Gratitude?

1	2	3	4	5

10. Do you Cultivate Contentment?

1	2	3	4	5

11. Do you Show Kindness?

1	2	3	4	5

12. Do you Persevere Through Adversity?

1	2	3	4	5

13. Do you Pursue Justice?

1	2	3	4	5

14. Do you Seek Harmony?

1	2	3	4	5

15. Do you Develop Self Awareness?

1	2	3	4	5

16. Do you Live with Balance?

1	2	3	4	5

17. Do you Practice Compassion?

1	2	3	4	5

18. Do you Respect Our Elders?

1	2	3	4	5

19. Do you Share Joy and Laughter?

1	2	3	4	5

20. Do you Enjoy Healthy Humor?

1	2	3	4	5

21. Do you Serve with Love?

1	2	3	4	5

Low Score: 21-38

Thank you for being honest with yourself. Acknowledgment and awareness are important first steps.

Pick one or two principles that are most important to you and focus on them for the next week. Think about the way you currently behave and contrast that to your aspirational behavior. Write down three situations where you may have the opportunity to exhibit these behaviors and then for each principle you selected, write a statement describing how you will handle the situation when it comes up in real life. By thinking through this in advance, you have a pre-determined response that will allow you to react quickly and in alignment with the principle you wish to embrace. Keep going and never give up on yourself. With a focused effort you can develop into the person that you want to be!

Below Average Score: 39-54

There is still a lot of room for improvement, but you are making good progress. You have strengths that are recognized by others, and you really shine in some areas. Life is a journey from being selfish to selfless. As you continue to embrace these principles in your life you will start to feel a change. You will begin to think more about how your behaviors affect others around you. As you continue to focus on installing good habits and behaviors people will notice the change in you. This positive reinforcement will help you to continue to move forward in your personal development. Enjoy the journey and give yourself some grace when you fall short. You are on your way!

Average Score: 55-72

You are getting there, keep going! You have become more aware of your behaviors in various situations and are making intentional efforts to improve. Being aware of your behaviors will allow you continue to make changes and progress along the path to being a conscientious and well-rounded adult in all areas of your life. You have developed many personal strengths that other recognize and admire. You are getting clear on the person that you intend to be. You know you are making progress, and you feel that you can continue to improve because of the progress you have made so far. Those closest to you need you to be the best you can be, and they also recognize your progress. Your personal development is happening in real time!

Above Average Score: 73-90

You are developing a reputation for being a good person in many areas of your life. You can be relied on in most situations to do the right thing. You still have a couple of areas where there is room for improvement. By focusing on the areas where you fall a little short you can complete your transformation into a role model for others to follow. Identify someone who has mastered the principle that you need to improve. Analyze how they behave when confronted with a choice to embrace a correct principle. Follow their example the next time you are faced with a similar choice. People are noticing your personal development and look up to you as an example. Keep up the good work!

High Score: 91-105

Great job! You are an example to all of us. Consistently applying these principles has proven to be a blessing in your life. People can trust you and rely on you. You have shown that you are a good person of high moral character. As someone who leads by example, you have credibility with others, even those who may not agree with you. They will respect you for being firm in following the principles you value. You have an opportunity to lead and teach others. People are watching you more than you know. You have become a well-rounded adult. Continue to shine your light so that others can follow!

Take the Online 21 Principles Personal Assessment

ENGAGED PATRI☆TS

FAMILY ASSESSMENT TOOL

Instructions: The following assessment is designed to provide feedback on how you can strengthen your family. Please answer each question truthfully and accurately. Choose the option that best describes your family's current behaviors, attitudes, or beliefs.

Scoring: Please rate each question on a scale of 1 to 5, with 5 being the highest score.

1 - Never / Not Applicable
2 - Rarely
3 - Sometimes
4 - Often
5 - Always

Communication

Do family members talk to each other about their feelings, thoughts, and concerns?

1	2	3	4	5

Do family members take the time to actively listen to one another?

1	2	3	4	5

Does your family communicate effectively, responding to one another in a timely and respectful manner?

1	2	3	4	5

Does your family practice open communication, even with tough topics or disagreements?

1	2	3	4	5

Do family members feel safe sharing their secrets with each other?

1	2	3	4	5

Support

Do family members encourage and support each other?

1	2	3	4	5

Do family members help each other with school/work projects?

Family Assessment Tool

1	2	3	4	5

Do family members listen when someone is upset or having a hard time?

1	2	3	4	5

Do family members have regular hugs or displays of affection toward each other?

1	2	3	4	5

Do family members make sacrifices for each other?

1	2	3	4	5

Time Together

Does your family have regular meals together?

1	2	3	4	5

Does your family spend quality time together on a regular basis?

1	2	3	4	5

Do you and your family have regular family movie nights or game nights?

1	2	3	4	5

Do you and your family vacation together?

1	2	3	4	5

Do you and your family spend holidays together?

1	2	3	4	5

Boundaries

Does your family have clear and respected boundaries?

1	2	3	4	5

Does the family respect each other's boundaries with grandparents or other relatives?

1	2	3	4	5

Do family members respect each other's privacy and personal space?

1	2	3	4	5

Does your family have established rules and expectations that are followed by all members?

1	2	3	4	5

Are family members given equal opportunities and responsibilities?

1	2	3	4	5

Gratitude and Forgiveness

Does the family hold grudges toward each other?

1	2	3	4	5

Are family members encouraged to say thank you and show appreciation toward each other?

1	2	3	4	5

Family Assessment Tool

Does the family give gifts or do kind gestures for each other on special occasions?

1	2	3	4	5

Does your family practice mutual respect, especially during disagreements or differing opinions?

1	2	3	4	5

Do family members apologize when they make mistakes?

1	2	3	4	5

Shared Values

Does your family share similar values and beliefs?

1	2	3	4	5

Are family members encouraged to share their opinions and beliefs with one another?

1	2	3	4	5

Do you live your family values consistently?

1	2	3	4	5

Can your neighbors determine your family values based on your actions?

1	2	3	4	5

Do your family values guide your daily actions?

1	2	3	4	5

Flexibility

Does your family accept change and adapt to new situations easily?

1	2	3	4	5

Does your family handle a change in plan, such as rescheduling a family event with ease?

1	2	3	4	5

Does your family embrace new ideas and new members easily?

1	2	3	4	5

Is your family comfortable with spontaneous activities?

1	2	3	4	5

Do you feel your family is handles surprises well?

1	2	3	4	5

Categories:
Communication (Questions 1-5)
Support (Questions 6-10)
Time Together (Questions 11-15)
Boundaries (Questions 16-20)
Gratitude and Forgiveness (Questions 21-25)
Shared Values (Questions 26-30)
Flexibility (Questions 31-35)

Weighted Scoring for Each Category:
1-5 = Low Score
6-10 = Below Average Score
11-15 = Average Score
16-20 = Above Average Score
21-25 = High Score

Overall Scoring:
1-35 = Low Score
36-70 = Below Average Score
71-105 = Average Score
106-140 = Above Average Score
141-175 = High Score

Communication

Low Score:
- Seek professional help from a therapist or counselor to learn effective communication skills.
- Practice active listening and validate each other's feelings.
- Avoid interrupting or dismissing each other's opinions.

Below Average Score:
- Schedule regular family meetings to discuss important issues.

- Use "I" statements instead of "you" statements when expressing concerns.
- Practice positive communication by giving compliments and expressing gratitude.

Average Score:

- Continue to practice active listening and use nonverbal cues to show understanding.
- Encourage open and honest communication by creating a safe and nonjudgmental environment.
- Practice effective conflict resolution skills, such as compromise and negotiation.

Above Average Score:

- Continue to communicate openly and honestly with each other.
- Practice assertive communication by expressing your needs and boundaries respectfully.
- Encourage each other to express their thoughts and feelings freely.

High Score:

- Keep up the great communication and continue to prioritize it in your family.
- Celebrate each other's communication strengths and use them to build stronger connections.
- Practice regular communication check-ins to maintain healthy communication habits.

Family Assessment Tool

Support

Low Score:

- Seek professional help from a therapist or counselor to address any underlying issues that may be affecting support.
- Identify the areas where support is lacking and work together to find solutions.
- Practice empathy and understanding toward each other's needs and struggles.

Below Average Score:

- Schedule regular check-ins with each other to offer emotional support.
- Practice active listening and offer validation and encouragement.
- Look for ways to help each other in practical ways, such as running errands or completing chores.

Average Score:

- Continue to offer emotional and practical support to each other.
- Practice self-care to avoid burnout and maintain a healthy balance.
- Be mindful of each other's boundaries and ask for consent before offering support.

Above Average Score:

- Celebrate each other's strengths and support each other's goals and dreams.

- Practice gratitude by expressing appreciation for the support you receive.
- Look for opportunities to offer support to others outside of the family.

High Score:
- Keep up the excellent support and continue to prioritize it in your family.
- Practice active listening and offer validation and encouragement.
- Celebrate each other's accomplishments and milestones.

Time Together

Low Score:
- Schedule regular quality time together to build stronger connections.
- Plan fun activities and outings to do together.
- Eliminate distractions, such as phones or TV during family time.

Below Average Score:
- Schedule regular family dinners or game nights.
- Make time for one-on-one activities with each family member.
- Be present and engaged during family time by actively participating.

Average Score:
- Continue to prioritize quality time together.
- Try new activities or hobbies together to keep things interesting.
- Set aside designated time for family bonding, such as vacations or staycations.

Above Average Score:
- Continue to make family time a priority and plan regular activities and outings.
- Look for opportunities to deepen your family connections, such as by having meaningful conversations or trying new experiences together.
- Encourage each other to maintain a healthy work/life balance and prioritize family time.

High Score:
- Keep up the great work with spending quality time together.
- Plan regular family activities and outings to create more memories.
- Encourage each other to prioritize family time and make it a priority in your busy lives.

Boundaries

Low Score:
- Establish clear boundaries and communicate them to each other.

- Respect each other's boundaries, even if you don't agree with them.
- Seek professional help from a therapist or counselor to address boundary issues.

Below Average Score:
- Continue to establish clear boundaries and communicate them to each other.
- Practice empathy and understanding toward each other's boundaries.
- Create consequences for crossing boundaries and follow through with them.

Average Score:
- Maintain and reinforce established boundaries.
- Continuously communicate and adjust boundaries as needed.
- Practice respect and understanding toward each other's boundaries.

Above Average Score:
- Celebrate each other's ability to establish and maintain healthy boundaries.
- Continue to communicate and adjust boundaries as needed.
- Support each other in maintaining boundaries with others outside of the family.

High Score:

- Keep up the great boundary-setting and continue to prioritize it in your family.

- Celebrate each other's ability to respect and maintain boundaries.

- Practice boundary setting in other areas of your life to maintain healthy relationships.

Gratitude and Forgiveness

Low Score:

- Practice active listening and validate each other's feelings.

- Seek professional help from a therapist or counselor to address forgiveness and gratitude issues.

- Practice empathy and understanding toward each other's needs and struggles.

Below Average Score:

- Practice expressing gratitude by giving compliments and expressing appreciation.

- Practice forgiveness by letting go of grudges and resentments.

- Practice empathy and understanding toward each other's perspectives.

Average Score:

- Continue to practice gratitude and forgiveness toward each other.

- Practice expressing gratitude and forgiveness, even in small moments.
- Look for opportunities to express gratitude and forgiveness outside of the family.

Above Average Score:
- Celebrate each other's ability to express gratitude and forgiveness.
- Continue to practice expressing gratitude and forgiveness regularly.
- Encourage each other to practice gratitude and forgiveness in all areas of their lives.

High Score:
- Keep up the great work with expressing gratitude and forgiveness.
- Celebrate each other's strengths in expressing gratitude and forgiveness.
- Practice expressing gratitude and forgiveness toward others outside of the family.

Shared Values

Low Score:
- Identify and communicate your individual values.
- Seek professional help from a therapist or counselor to address value conflicts.
- Practice active listening and empathy toward each other's values.

Below Average Score:
- Identify and discuss shared values as a family.
- Encourage each other to live by shared values.
- Practice empathy and understanding toward each other's values.

Average Score:
- Continue to live by shared values as a family.
- Encourage each other to make decisions based on shared values.
- Practice open communication and empathy toward each other's values.

Above Average Score:
- Celebrate each other's ability to live by shared values.
- Encourage each other to incorporate shared values in all areas of their lives.
- Practice empathy and understanding toward those who may not share your family's values.

High Score:
- Keep up the great work with sharing common values and beliefs.
- Continuously discuss and review shared values to ensure they remain aligned.
- Encourage each other to act on shared values in everyday life.

Flexibility

Low Score:
- Practice active listening and open communication to understand each other's perspectives.
- Practice empathy and understanding toward each other's needs and wants.
- Seek professional help from a therapist or counselor to address flexibility issues.

Below Average Score:
- Practice compromise and finding common ground.
- Be open to trying new things and considering different perspectives.
- Practice empathy and understanding toward each other's limitations.

Average Score:
- Continue to practice compromise and being open to new ideas.
- Practice flexibility in everyday situations.
- Communicate clearly and respectfully when expressing needs and wants.

Above Average Score:
- Celebrate each other's ability to be flexible.
- Encourage each other to embrace change and be open to new experiences.
- Practice flexibility in other areas of your life.

Family Assessment Tool

High Score:

- Keep up the great work with being flexible.
- Celebrate each other's strengths in being adaptable.
- Encourage each other to lead by example in practicing flexibility in all areas of life.

Take the Online Family Assessment

ENGAGED PATRI☆TS

SPIRITUALITY ASSESSMENT

Instructions: The following assessment is designed to measure an individual's level of spirituality and worship. Please answer each question truthfully and accurately. Choose the option that best describes your current behavior, attitude, or belief.

Scoring: Please rate each question on a scale of 1 to 5, with 5 being the highest score.

1 - Never / Not Applicable
2 - Rarely
3 - Sometimes
4 - Often
5 - Always

Spirituality Assessment

Personal Habits and Practices

How often do you read the Bible or other spiritual texts?

1	2	3	4	5

To what extent do you engage in daily prayer, meditation, or devotional practices?

1	2	3	4	5

How consistently do you attend religious services or gatherings?

1	2	3	4	5

Do you regularly practice acts of service or charity?

1	2	3	4	5

How frequently do you experience feelings of gratitude and appreciation for your blessings?

1	2	3	4	5

Relationship with God

How much do you trust in God's guidance and providence?

1	2	3	4	5

How often do you experience a deep sense of connection or communion with God?

1	2	3	4	5

How often do you feel a sense of purpose, meaning, or direction aligned with your faith?

1	2	3	4	5

Are you confident in your spiritual beliefs?

1	2	3	4	5

Do you prioritize and align your life with God's values and principles?

1	2	3	4	5

Relationship with Others

Do you consistently forgive and show compassion toward others?

1	2	3	4	5

Are you respectful of others who differ from your beliefs or worldview?

1	2	3	4	5

Are you respectful of other's spiritual beliefs and practices?

1	2	3	4	5

Are you generous with your time, attention, and resources to those in need or struggling?

1	2	3	4	5

Spirituality Assessment

Do you foster positive relationships and pursue reconciliation with those who have offended or mistreated you?

1	2	3	4	5

Character and Behavior

Do you practice self-control over harmful habits or tendencies?

1	2	3	4	5

Are you honest and truthful in your dealings with others?

1	2	3	4	5

Do you live the virtues, of humility, patience, courage, and perseverance?

1	2	3	4	5

Do you react positively in response to difficult life situations, suffering, or hardships?

1	2	3	4	5

Do you experience inner peace, joy, and contentment?

1	2	3	4	5

Categories:
Personal Habits and Practices (Questions 1-5)
Relationship with God (Questions 6-10)
Relationship with Others (Questions 11-15)
Character and Behavior (Questions 16-20)

Weighted Scoring:
20-36 = Low Score
37-52 = Below Average Score
53-68 = Average Score
69-84 = Above Average Score
85-100 = High Score

Recommendations

Low Scores:

- Develop a consistent daily practice of prayer, meditation, or devotion.
- Prioritize attending church or religious gatherings regularly.
- Engage in acts of service, generosity, and charity toward others.

Below Average Scores:

- Seek to deepen your understanding of your faith through study and reflection.

- Attend a spiritual retreat or conference to renew and refresh your faith.
- Seek out a mentor or spiritual guide to provide support and guidance.

Average Scores:

- Identify areas where you can improve and set specific goals to grow in your faith.
- Make a habit of daily reflection and gratitude, focusing on your spiritual blessings.
- Find ways to serve and love others in your daily life.

Above Average Scores:

- Keep up the good work and continue to deepen and enrich your spiritual practices.
- Share your faith and positive spiritual experiences with others.
- Seek out opportunities to engage in acts of service and outreach to those in need.

High Scores:

- Share your faith and serve as a mentor or spiritual guide to others.
- Maintain a healthy balance between spiritual practices and daily life.
- Keep growing and seeking new ways to deepen your relationship with God and others.

Take the Online Spirituality Assessment.
It includes additional recommendations

DECLARATION OF INDEPENDENCE

In Congress, July 4, 1776

The unanimous Declaration of the thirteen United States of America, When in the Course of human events, it becomes necessary for one people to dissolve the political bands which have connected them with another, and to assume among the powers of the earth, the separate and equal station to which the Laws of Nature and of Nature's God entitle them, a decent respect to the opinions of mankind requires that they should declare the causes which impel them to the separation.

We hold these truths to be self-evident, that all men are created equal, that they are endowed by their Creator with certain unalienable Rights, that among these are Life, Liberty and the pursuit of Happiness.--That to secure these rights, Governments are instituted among Men, deriving their just powers from the consent of the governed, --That whenever any Form of Government becomes destructive of these ends, it is the Right of the People to alter or to abolish it, and to institute new Government, laying its foundation on such principles and organizing its powers in such form, as to them shall seem most likely to effect their Safety and Happiness. Prudence, indeed, will dictate that Governments long established should not be changed for light and transient causes; and accordingly all experience hath shewn, that mankind are more disposed to suffer, while evils are sufferable, than to right themselves by abolishing the forms to which they are accustomed. But when a long train of abuses and usurpations, pursuing invariably the same Object evinces a design to reduce them under absolute Despotism, it is their right, it is their duty, to throw off such Government, and to provide new Guards for their future security. -- Such has been the patient sufferance of these Colonies; and such is now the necessity which constrains them to alter their former Systems of Government. The history of the present King of Great Britain is a history of repeated injuries and usurpations, all having in direct object the establishment of an absolute Tyranny over these States. To prove this, let Facts be submitted to a candid world.

He has refused his Assent to Laws, the most wholesome and necessary for the public good.

He has forbidden his Governors to pass Laws of immediate and pressing importance, unless suspended in their operation till his Assent should be obtained; and when so suspended, he has utterly neglected to attend to them.

He has refused to pass other Laws for the accommodation of large districts of people, unless those people would relinquish the right of Representation in the Legislature, a right inestimable to them and formidable to tyrants only.

He has called together legislative bodies at places unusual, uncomfortable, and distant from the depository of their public Records, for the sole purpose of fatiguing them into compliance with his measures.

He has dissolved Representative Houses repeatedly, for opposing with manly firmness his invasions on the rights of the people.

He has refused for a long time, after such dissolutions, to cause others to be elected; whereby the Legislative powers, incapable of Annihilation, have returned to the People at large for their exercise; the State remaining in the meantime exposed to all the dangers of invasion from without, and convulsions within.

He has endeavoured to prevent the population of these States; for that purpose, obstructing the Laws for Naturalization of Foreigners; refusing to pass others to encourage their migrations hither, and raising the conditions of new Appropriations of Lands.

He has obstructed the Administration of Justice, by refusing his Assent to Laws for establishing Judiciary powers.

He has made Judges dependent on his Will alone, for the tenure of their offices, and the amount and payment of their salaries.

He has erected a multitude of New Offices and sent hither swarms of Officers to harrass our people, and eat out their substance.

He has kept among us, in times of peace, Standing Armies without the Consent of our legislatures.

He has affected to render the Military independent of and superior to the Civil power.

He has combined with others to subject us to a jurisdiction foreign to our constitution, and unacknowledged by our laws; giving his Assent to their Acts of pretended Legislation:

For Quartering large bodies of armed troops among us:

For protecting them, by a mock Trial, from punishment for any Murders which they should commit on the Inhabitants of these States:

For cutting off our Trade with all parts of the world:

For imposing Taxes on us without our Consent:

For depriving us in many cases, of the benefits of Trial by Jury:

For transporting us beyond Seas to be tried for pretended offences

For abolishing the free System of English Laws in a neighbouring Province, establishing therein an Arbitrary government, and enlarging its Boundaries so as to render it at once an example and fit instrument for introducing the same absolute rule into these Colonies:

For taking away our Charters, abolishing our most valuable Laws, and altering fundamentally the Forms of our Governments:

For suspending our own Legislatures, and declaring themselves invested with power to legislate for us in all cases whatsoever.

He has abdicated Government here, by declaring us out of his Protection and waging War against us.

He has plundered our seas, ravaged our Coasts, burnt our towns, and destroyed the lives of our people.

He is at this time transporting large Armies of foreign Mercenaries to compleat the works of death, desolation and tyranny, already begun with circumstances of Cruelty & perfidy scarcely paralleled in the most barbarous ages, and totally unworthy the Head of a civilized nation.

He has constrained our fellow Citizens taken Captive on the high Seas to bear Arms against their Country, to become the executioners of their friends and Brethren, or to fall themselves by their Hands.

He has excited domestic insurrections amongst us, and has endeavoured to bring on the inhabitants of our frontiers, the merciless Indian Savages, whose known rule of warfare, is an undistinguished destruction of all ages, sexes and conditions.

In every stage of these Oppressions We have Petitioned for Redress in the most humble terms: Our repeated Petitions have been answered only by repeated injury. A Prince whose character is thus marked by every act which may define a Tyrant, is unfit to be the ruler of a free people.

Nor have We been wanting in attentions to our Brittish brethren. We have warned them from time to time of attempts by their legislature to extend an unwarrantable jurisdiction over us. We have reminded them of the circumstances of our emigration and settlement here. We have appealed to their native justice and magnanimity, and we have conjured them by the ties of our common kindred to disavow these usurpations, which, would inevitably interrupt our connections and correspondence. They too have been deaf to the voice of justice and of consanguinity. We must, therefore, acquiesce in the necessity, which denounces our Separation, and hold them, as we hold the rest of mankind, Enemies in War, in Peace Friends.

We, therefore, the Representatives of the united States of America, in General Congress, Assembled, appealing to the Supreme Judge of the world for the rectitude of our intentions, do, in the Name, and by Authority of the good People of these Colonies, solemnly publish and declare, That these United Colonies are, and of Right ought to be Free and Independent States; that they are Absolved from all Allegiance to the British Crown, and that all political connection between them and the State of Great Britain, is and ought to be totally dissolved; and that as Free and Independent States, they have full Power to levy War, conclude Peace, contract Alliances, establish Commerce, and to do all other Acts and Things which Independent States may of right do. And for the support of this Declaration, with a firm reliance on the protection of divine Providence, we mutually pledge to each other our Lives, our Fortunes and our sacred Honor.

Georgia

Button Gwinnett

Lyman Hall

George Walton

North Carolina

William Hooper

Joseph Hewes

John Penn

South Carolina

Edward Rutledge

Thomas Heyward, Jr.

Thomas Lynch, Jr.

Arthur Middleton

Massachusetts

John Hancock

Maryland

Samuel Chase

William Paca

Thomas Stone

Charles Carroll of Carrollton

Virginia

George Wythe

Richard Henry Lee

Thomas Jefferson

Benjamin Harrison

Thomas Nelson, Jr.

Francis Lightfoot Lee

Carter Braxton

Lewis Morris

Pennsylvania

Robert Morris

Benjamin Rush

Benjamin Franklin

John Morton

George Clymer

James Smith

George Taylor

James Wilson

George Ross

Delaware

Caesar Rodney

George Read

Thomas McKean

New York

William Floyd

Philip Livingston

Francis Lewis

New Jersey

Richard Stockton

John Witherspoon

Francis Hopkinson

John Hart

Abraham Clark

New Hampshire

Josiah Bartlett

William Whipple

Massachusetts

Samuel Adams

John Adams

Robert Treat Paine

Elbridge Gerry

Rhode Island

Stephen Hopkins

Declaration of Independence

William Ellery

William Williams

Oliver Wolcott

Connecticut

Roger Sherman

New Hampshire

Samuel Huntington

Matthew Thornton

BILL OF RIGHTS

Original Ten Amendments: The Bill of Rights
Passed by Congress September 25, 1789.
Ratified December 15, 1791.

AMENDMENT I

Congress shall make no law respecting an establishment of religion, or prohibiting the free exercise thereof; or abridging the freedom of speech, or of the press, or the right of the people peaceably to assemble, and to petition the Government for a redress of grievances.

AMENDMENT II

A well regulated Militia, being necessary to the security of a free State, the right of the people to keep and bear Arms, shall not be infringed.

AMENDMENT III

No Soldier shall, in time of peace be quartered in any house, without the consent of the Owner, nor in time of war, but in a manner to be prescribed by law.

AMENDMENT IV

Bill of Rights

The right of the people to be secure in their persons, houses, papers, and effects, against unreasonable searches and seizures, shall not be violated, and no Warrants shall issue, but upon probable cause, supported by Oath or affirmation, and particularly describing the place to be searched, and the persons or things to be seized.

Amendment V

No person shall be held to answer for a capital, or otherwise infamous crime, unless on a presentment or indictment of a Grand Jury, except in cases arising in the land or naval forces, or in the Militia, when in actual service in time of War or public danger; nor shall any person be subject for the same offence to be twice put in jeopardy of life or limb, nor shall be compelled in any criminal case to be a witness against himself, nor be deprived of life, liberty, or property, without due process of law; nor shall private property be taken for public use, without just compensation.

Amendment VI

In all criminal prosecutions, the accused shall enjoy the right to a speedy and public trial, by an impartial jury of the State and district wherein the crime shall have been committed; which district shall have been previously ascertained by law, and to be informed of the nature and cause of the accusation; to be confronted with the witnesses against him; to have compulsory process for obtaining witnesses in his favor, and to have the assistance of counsel for his defense.

Amendment VII

In Suits at common law, where the value in controversy shall exceed twenty dollars, the right of trial by jury shall be preserved, and no fact tried by a jury shall be otherwise re-examined in any Court of the United States, than according to the rules of the common law.

AMENDMENT VIII

Excessive bail shall not be required, nor excessive fines imposed, nor cruel and unusual punishments inflicted.

AMENDMENT IX

The enumeration in the Constitution of certain rights shall not be construed to deny or disparage others retained by the people.

AMENDMENT X

The powers not delegated to the United States by the Constitution, nor prohibited by it to the States, are reserved to the States respectively, or to the people.

ENGAGED PATRI★TS

So, ASK YOURSELF THE FOLLOWING

QUESTIONS:

1. Are you a Patriot?
2. Are you tired of the Woke Agenda?
3. Are you concerned our Freedoms are at risk?
4. Do you want to make a difference?
5. Will you leave your family a legacy of Freedom?
6. Are you ready to lead?

If your answers to these questions are 100% YES,
then you have found your people!

Who are our people **- Patriots**

Who are not our people **- Woke Liberals**

What is our Cause **- Saving Freedom for Future Generations**

What is our Vision **- Convert the Silent Moral Majority into Engaged Patriots**

What are our Core Values **- The 10 value declarations in the Engaged Patriots Manifesto**

`

What is our Mission - **Help Patriots embrace and live the 10 Declarations in the Engaged Patriots Manifesto**

What is our Strategy - **Create a thriving community where Patriots can learn, engage, and Work Together to Strengthen our Families and Communities**

Join us!

Every added member strengthens our resolve and increases our impact in the world.

Transform your world from the inside out. Start with you and expand to your family and community

My name is Matthew J Cameron. I am not an Author. I am not a Writer. I am not Famous. I am a Son, Brother, Husband, Father, Grandfather, and Patriot. I felt compelled to write this book. It comes from my heart. I wrote it for my children and grandchildren.

I was tired of all the woke agenda pushing their corrupt immoral values on us. I was tired of my innocent grandchildren being exposed to their evil ways. I sat idly by as many great patriots stepped up and shared their beliefs and encouraged other Patriots to embrace the cause of Freedom. My conscience worked on me and I knew I needed to do more than watch others carry the yoke. I hope you will find this little book to be a source of encouragement and strength for you and your family. I. hope that you will embrace the declarations in the manifesto and choose to be a more Engaged Patriot. The ten declarations in the Engaged Patriot Manifesto are based on common sense and time-tested principles. They are a statement of conservative values and a proposed action plan, that can serve as a guide in our daily lives.

The world needs more good people to step up and increase their personal influence. You are stronger than you think, and your unique influence and leadership is desperately needed today!

To Our Freedom!

Ingram Content Group UK Ltd.
Milton Keynes UK
UKHW021846100723
424887UK00021B/309/J

9 798988 318514